TEACHING GERMAN

A BLAISDELL BOOK IN THE MODERN LANGUAGES

Henry H. H. Remak, *Indiana University*
CONSULTING EDITOR

TEACHING GERMAN
A Linguistic Orientation

ROBERT L. POLITZER
Stanford University

BLAISDELL PUBLISHING COMPANY
A Division of Ginn and Company
WALTHAM, MASSACHUSETTS · TORONTO · LONDON

Foreword

Like its companion volumes *Teaching French* and *Teaching Spanish*, this book deals primarily with imparting the basic skills to students on the high school or college levels. The emphasis of the book is on the application of linguistic principles to teaching, rather than on the development of techniques of linguistic analysis.

The aim of the book is not to teach German, but to show how linguistic analysis and principles may be utilized in the teaching of German. The reader of the book is assumed to have a good knowledge of German. The purpose of this work is to systematize this knowledge, to point out the conflicts of patterns between English and German, and to suggest practical solutions. *The Sounds of English and German* and *The Grammatical Structures of English and German*, which have appeared in the Contrastive Structure Series sponsored by the Modern Language Association Center of Applied Linguistics, present some of the material and problems of this book. So does the manual *Applied Linguistics, German*, which forms part of the series originally sponsored by the United States Office of Education. My presentation is, I hope, less technical and, as the title of this book indicates, closer to the problems of teaching. I trust that the reader of this book will find it possible to consult all of the resource material that recent advances in linguistics and teaching methodology put at our disposal.

Part I of this book (especially Chapters II and IIIA) follows closely the corresponding sections of *Teaching French* and *Teaching Spanish*. Recent controversy in foreign-language teaching methodology has centered on what has been called the clash between an audio-lingual habit theory and a cognitive code theory of language learning. I have, in fact, always held that language teaching in the classroom must take into account both of these theories and approaches to language learning. Those familiar with *Teaching French* and *Teaching Spanish* will recognize that this book stresses the cognitive code theory more than its predecessors. There are two complementary reasons for this increased stress on a cognitive code type of approach: (1) I feel that in recent years the audio-lingual habit theory—badly in need of emphasis, let us say, ten or fifteen years ago—has been overstressed by some teachers who are overconfident of the results of memorization and automatization. (2) It seems to me that the mastery of a highly inflected language like German by a native speaker of English presupposes conscious control of some structural patterns to an even larger degree than in the case of either French or Spanish.

I am very grateful to all my colleagues who have contributed suggestions and criticism, and especially to Professor Henry H. H. Remak for his valuable advice and his careful readings of the manuscript.

RLP

Stanford University, 1967

Contents

PART ONE

CHAPTER I

Linguistics and Applied Linguistics

(A) THE LINGUIST'S VIEW OF LANGUAGE

All languages are systems used for communication. Although many languages have been reduced to written form, all human languages are primarily systems utilizing the medium of the human voice. Thus the sounds that our vocal organs are capable of producing are the material that languages are made of. The human voice is, of course, capable of producing many sounds, but only a few of those many sounds are utilized by any one language.

We may think of a language as a set of building stones out of which we can "construct" utterances. All speakers of a language know the rules according to which the building stones may be put together into constructions. They all know that certain constructions express certain meanings. The sounds that a given language has chosen are the smallest units, the smallest building stones with which this language operates. All other building stones are created by combining or recombining these smallest building stones—the so-called **phonemes**—into different sequences.

The phonemes operate on a very simple principle. Each phoneme of a language must be different from any other phoneme of the same language, and the speaker must know how to **perceive** and **produce** this difference. The fact that a native speaker of English can make and hear the difference between the initial sounds of *pit* and *bit* proves that the *p* and *b* sounds are distinct phonemes of English. (Conventionally linguists express this by writing /p/ and /b/ between slanted lines.) In the same way, the fact that German has words like *nackt* and *Nacht* proves that the sounds expressed by the letters *ck* and *ch* (namely the sounds /k/ and /x/) are phonemes of German.

Sounds that are different from each other and used within the same language system are not necessarily different phonemes. First of all, the human voice is not really capable of always producing the same sound in exactly the same way. If you repeat the word *pit* ten times, you are likely to vary the pronunciation of each sound. You do not really say the identical sound ten times, but the variation is accidental. It is of the type that will be ignored by the native speaker, though at times it can happen that the non-native will pick up and be confused by these accidental variations that occur within the speech of the same individual—and perhaps occur even more frequently from one individual to another. Other nonsignificant (**nonphonemic**) differences between sounds are predictable and follow distinct patterns. Thus the *p*-sound of English *pit* is not the same *p*-sound used in English *spit*. The sound of *pit* is followed by a slight puff of air (**aspiration**), which is absent in the *p* of *spit*. However, the absence of the puff of air always accompanies the preceding *s*. Whenever the *s* precedes the sound *p* (as in *spit*, *spot*, *spike*), the puff of air is absent. This is another way of saying that the *p* without the puff of air exists only in positions in which the *p* with the puff of air does not exist. They are in "complementary" distribution. Therefore, they are not used to distinguish words. They are only variations of each other. In order to be able to distinguish words, they would have to be capable of occurring in exactly the same position (as /p/ and /b/ in *pit* and *bit*). They would have to be in "contrastive distribution." All sounds that are different from each other but not in contrastive distribution are thus really variants (technical name: **allophones**) of the same phoneme. Allophones of the same phoneme are usually quite similar to each other—or at least they sound similar to the native speaker of the language. To the native of English, the /p/ of *pit* sounds very much like the /p/ of *spit*; to the ears of a speaker of a language that utilizes these two sounds as phonemes in contrastive distribution, for example, distinguishing a word *pa* (no puff of air after *p*) from a word *pha* (with puff of air), the two sounds are sometimes very different. Differences between allophones can be considerable. The German phoneme /r/ at the beginning of the word (*richtig*) is pronounced very differently from the way in which it appears at the end of the word (*sehr*). Still, since the one pronunciation can never contrast with the other in the same position, these two very different sounds (which occur at the beginning of *richtig* and at the end of *sehr*) are variants, or allophones, of the same phoneme.

Phonemes can be combined into larger units. Most laymen would probably assume that the units next in size to the phoneme are the syllables. In a sense this is correct; but syllables are units created by the alternation of sounds in the stream of speech, rather than building stones of the language system. As we speak, sounds produced with a great deal of power alternate with other sounds produced with less power. Typically, each sound that represents a peak of voice power (usually a vowel) joins with the neighboring less powerful sounds to form a syllable. Within the linguistic system, however, the units next in size to the phoneme seem to be of a slightly different nature. In order to isolate these units, let us compare three German sentences:

1. *Wir arbeiten immer mit deinem Bruder.*
2. *Wir sprechen mit seinem Vater.*
3. *Karl spricht mit diesem Arbeiter.*

What are the smallest units (above the phoneme level) into which these sentences can be dissected? As we stated above, we are not speaking about syllables. If we compare them carefully, our sentences give at least one example of a unit that is smaller than a syllable and is nevertheless a constant, usable and reusable building stone of German—namely the *t* at the end of *spricht,* which is the *t* of the third person and is obviously the same third-person marker that appears in *sagt, lacht,* and *arbeitet.* Also we should note that the *t* of *spricht, sagt,* and *lacht* is to be distinguished from the *t* of *Tag, Arbeit,* and *Teller* because the *t* of these latter words does not have a clearly marked function or meaning. The *t* of those words is merely a phoneme, but the *t* of *lacht* and *spricht* is more than a phoneme: since it has an identifiable meaning or function, it is a linguistic unit of a higher level. It is a so-called **morpheme**—the smallest unit used with an identifiable meaning or function of its own. If we look at our examples more closely, we shall see that some of these units may be morphemes—for example, the *t* of *spricht*—and that some may be words or syllables or at any rate may be composed of several syllables. Thus *wir* is a word and at the same time a morpheme: it cannot be subdivided further into any unit having a particular meaning or function. *Arbeiten,* on the other hand, comes apart into the morpheme {*arbeit*} (re-used in Sentence 3 in *Arbeiter*) and the morpheme {*en*} (re-used in Sentence 2 in *sprech-en*), indicating the first person plural. (Note that many linguistic textbooks use small { } to indicate morphemes.) *Immer* seems to be a word and a morpheme at the same time; so does *mit.* *Deinem* is divisible into *dein* and *em* (*em* being re-used in *sein-em* and *dies-em*). *Bruder* does not seem divisible into two reusable parts. However, from the point of view of the present German system we could say that it is nevertheless made up of two morphemes: *Brud* (which appears only and uniquely in this particular word) and *er*, an ending that is typical of many German nouns.

Just as a phoneme can appear in different forms or variants (allophones), so it is also possible for a morpheme to have several forms (**allomorphs**). All allomorphs of the same morpheme must, of course, have the same meaning or function, and each allomorph must and can occur only in a specific position where the other ones are not possible. Sometimes the occurrence of the various allomorphs depends on the preceding or following sounds. The most obvious example of the occurrence of allomorphs conditioned by preceding sounds are the English plurals: the English noun plural is normally formed by adding an −*s*: *cat* ≠ *cats*. If the noun ends in *s* or *sh*, the plural is formed by −*es* [−əz]: *dish* ≠ *dishes*, *bus* ≠ *buses*. Thus we can say that −*es* [−əz] is an allomorph that depends on the preceding sound. Note again that it would not be used where the /s/ is found, at least not correctly. The plurals **dishs *[diss]* (add −*s* as in *cat* ≠ *cats*) and **cates* (add −*es* as in *dish* ≠ *dishes*) may be "committed" by a foreigner learning English—but they are not English.[1] Sometimes the occurrence of an allomorph is determined by the form with which it is used. In the three sample sentences above, we had two allomorphs of the German root for *speak*: {*sprech* + *en*} and {*sprich* + *t*}. Note again that they cannot be used in the same position: the allomorph {*sprech*} requires the {*en*} ending, the allomorph {*sprich*} requires the {*t*}. *Er *sprecht* (instead of *spricht*) is a familiar mistake of the learner in the elementary course—but it is not German.

Just as a morpheme must minimally contain at least one phoneme, but can be made up of several phonemes, so a word must contain at least one morpheme, but may also be made up of several morphemes. As a matter of fact, linguists have had difficulty establishing a clear-cut and unambiguous definition of what a "word" really is. This need not trouble us too much since the concept seems fairly clear in actual usage. One way of defining a word (in German or English at least) is to say that it is the smallest possible form that could normally be used by itself as an independent utterance.

Perhaps more important than the correct definition of "word" is the recognition that in many languages (certainly in English and German) words belong to two broad categories: those that carry the lexical mean-

---

[1] An asterisk (*) preceding a word or structure indicates a merely hypothetical or (as above) erroneous form.

ing, or content, of the utterance and those that—while often also carrying lexical meaning—serve the purpose of expressing or denoting grammatical pattern or relationship. Words can of course be combined into a great number of constructions, clauses, or phrases that form the highest levels of combinations of building stones of the language. Yet, although the possible number of phrases or clauses that can be composed is almost infinite, many phrases or clauses follow the same blueprint, or pattern. If we compare the two German sentences:

1. *Heute spricht der kleine Junge mit seinem Vater.*
and
2. *Jetzt arbeitet der kluge Student mit seinem Freund.*

we notice that they have certain elements in common. The adverbs (*heute, jetzt*), the adjectives (*kleine, kluge*), the verbs (*spricht, arbeitet*), and the nouns (*Junge, Vater; Student, Freund*) are all different, but the grammatical construction is the same. Therefore, if we remove the actual words, we are left with a skeleton: (adverb) (verb) *der* (adjective + *e*) (noun) *mit seinem* (noun). This skeleton identifies the blueprint, or pattern, that is, the construction of the sentences. This pattern comprises the sequence in which the words are used. We could not change the order of adverb and verb in the sentences above without changing the pattern. *Spricht heute* . . . or *arbeitet jetzt* . . . instead of *heute spricht* . . . and *jetzt arbeitet* . . . would turn our sentences into questions. The pattern also includes the endings—that is, the morphemes associated with the third person singular of the verb, the nominative, and the dative of the nouns and adjectives. Third, the pattern includes words like *du, mit*, and *seinem*, without which the pattern would fall apart. These words, which help to determine the pattern, so to speak, are the **function words** of the language. Just like the main parts of speech (nouns, adjectives, adverbs, verbs), the function words also can be divided into specific classes, primarily on the basis of whether they can replace each other in the same pattern. Thus in the sentence, *Heute spricht der kleine Junge mit seinem Vater*, without changing the basic pattern *seinem* could be replaced by *dem, diesem, jenem, einem, meinem, unserem*, and so on. All the words that could replace *seinem* belong to the same class, or category, of function words. In a similar way, *mit* could be replaced by *zu, bei*, or *von* without change in construction. Therefore these prepositions belong to the same class of function words as *mit*.

To summarize, we can compare languages to sets of building stones: the smallest of these stones are the phonemes. One or several typical phonemes make up a morpheme. One or several morphemes make up a word. Usually several words (sometimes only one word) make up utterances. The utterances follow certain patterns that are defined in terms of word order, endings, and function words. Of course, the purpose of the system is to express meaning. Meaning is found at all levels except the lowest: the phonemes serve to express meaning, but they have no meaning by themselves in isolation.

Another noteworthy feature of the language system is that, normally at least, there is no necessary, but only a conventional or arbitrary, relationship between the linguistic symbols and the meanings which they express. We say "normally at least" because there are a few exceptions: if we call a dog a "bow-wow" (imitating the noise that the dog makes) the word used for *dog* is indeed related to the concept. Sometimes we can also demonstrate that in the highest forms of linguistic expression—in literature, especially in poetry—certain words, phrases, and sequences of words may have been chosen in order to be directly (in other words, through their sound, rhythm, etc.) expressive of moods or ideas that are to be conveyed. But in normal speech the relation between the linguistic symbol and the meanings conveyed is arbitrary. The symbols function for the reason already mentioned, namely, because they are different from each other, and not because there is an inherent relationship between the symbol and its meaning. For instance, the German word for *hat* is *Hut*. If we changed the *h* to *g*, it would mean something else (*gut*), and if we changed the *u* to *a*, it would again change the meaning (*hat*). Consider the sequence of words in *Karl arbeitet*. If we changed it, we would express a question (*arbeitet Karl?*) and not a statement. Thus the question *why* (raised at times earnestly, at times jokingly, by the language student) is ultimately answered by the simple statement that within a linguistic system a particular means to express a certain meaning has evolved, and that that particular means functions within the system because it contrasts with other means which express different meanings. The only other way of approaching the question *why* is, of course, in historical terms: in other words, the German word for *father* is *Vater* because there was a Middle High German word *vater*, which goes back to the Old High German word *fater*, which in turn is derived from a Germanic **fátēr*, which must have its origin in an Indo-European word **patḗr*.

Thus any linguistic unit, any one of the building stones of our language construction, functions only within its particular system. It fits into the blueprints, or patterns, provided by the system. It can be perceived because it is different from other building stones, and it has its own unique meaning or potential of meanings because it covers, within the system, a very special area or a field of meaning. We could perhaps think of all the possible meanings that can be expressed as a vast field. Each linguistic building stone covers a specific part of this field; but it can cover only those parts that are not covered by other stones. (There are, of course, synonyms—words whose ranges of meaning partially overlap—but **absolute** synonyms are rare.) Thus, the potential meaning of a word ultimately depends on how the other stones of the set are covering the field. From these considerations it follows that it is highly unlikely (from the theoretical point of view, at least, practically impossible) that a building stone of one linguistic system will cover the same area as that of another. German *wissen* and English *know* will overlap in area, but they certainly do not cover the same areas. The area of German *wissen* is restricted by the word *kennen*, while English *know* has no such neighbor and can spread over a much larger area in the field of meaning.

It is therefore evident that a building stone of one language can never be equated with that of another. As a matter of fact, such equations are probably the most fundamental cause of error in foreign-language learning. They are least harmful when the equations are established with very concrete, definite concepts (names for animals, objects, etc.) that seem to cover obvious, clear-cut semantic fields. They are usually more confusing when less concrete areas of meaning are involved, and may cause embarrassment when they are established for **function words** that are used to establish **grammatical relationship** (grammatical meanings) rather than lexical meanings referring to objects, actions, and so on. In other words, the learner equating *dog* with *Hund* will probably make few mistakes because of this equation (even though he should not translate the expression *you lucky dog* literally). The learner who equates *know* and *wissen* produces a sentence that might cause embarrassment to himself and perhaps offend his listener: *Ich weiss die Antwort* for *I know the answer*, but *Ich *weiss Herrn Schmidt* for *I know Mr. Schmidt* instead of *Ich kenne Herrn Schmidt* is obviously incorrect.

The equation of *the* with *der* is responsible for errors for which no German teacher will feel a particular need for illustration.

Before turning to the question of the application of linguistics to teaching, we should also point out that linguistics implies not only a certain view of the nature of language but also a method of analysis or, as some linguists would say, "discovery procedures" to be used when we must find out about the grammar of an unknown language. Here it is important to keep in mind that linguistics—especially within the United

States—has always had firm roots in the departments of anthropology and to some extent in religious missionary activities. In other words, linguists were and are often concerned with writing grammars of languages that have never been analyzed or written before. The initial learning situation under such circumstances is quite necessarily audio-lingual (no writing exists as yet); the traditional grammatical categories in many instances may not fit the language to be studied and, in any event, they cannot be used in the process of analysis. Definitions like "the subject performs the action" or "the noun is a name for a place, person, or thing" may be of little help in establishing the grammar of a language if your only access to the grammar is via the utterances of a native "inform-ant." The only way in which the grammar can be approached is through observations and comparisons of the utterances themselves, and through the purely formal rules they give about the grammatical structure of the language. Thus, assuming for a moment that English is an unknown language to be investigated, we certainly could not arrive at the category of noun and verb through definitions like the one above for the noun, or for the verb through statements like "the verb denotes the action." Such definitions correspond at best in a very rough way to the general meaning of nouns or verbs. We say that in a sentence like *The take-off of the plane was delayed*, the word *take-off* is a noun, although it refers to an action. In our initial attack on English, we would isolate categories like "noun" and "verb" rather through the observation that there are certain words which can be preceded by *the*, that there are others which take the *-s* endings in the third person singular, and so on. And we would conclude that *boy* and *child* are both nouns because they can replace each other in utterances (*The boy knows the answer*; *The child knows the answer*); and we would similarly conclude that *expect* is a verb because it can replace *know* in a sentence (*The boy expects the answer*). Since our native inform-ant would reject as nonsensical the suggestion to use *expect* instead of *boy* or *child* (*The *expect knows the answer*), we would have pretty good evidence that *expect* cannot be used as a noun.

(B) THE MEANING OF "APPLIED LINGUISTICS"

During the past twenty years, the views of linguists have become an ever-increasing influence on language instruction at all levels. The first major impact of linguistics upon language teaching occurred during World War II, when linguists were asked to create grammars of languages that had never or seldom been taught before (at least in the United States) and to teach those languages to military personnel. Another avenue through which the impact of linguists upon language teaching was felt came through the teaching of English as a foreign language. Again, it was primarily during and after World War II that an ever-increasing number of military personnel and students came to the United States. These foreigners were in need of acquiring as quickly as possible a practical command of American English, and linguists played an essential part in preparing the materials to be used in the teaching of American English. Through these two avenues, the linguistic view of language teaching spread first into the college curriculum, and from there into the teaching of foreign languages in the high schools.

Before enumerating some of the relationships of linguistics to language teaching, we want to underline one fact: applied linguistics relates to linguistics in approximately the way in which any applied science field relates to the science itself. An engineer must know applied mathematics and applied physics in order to build bridges; but he cannot and should not expect the mathematician or physicist to tell him what bridges to build in a particular situation. In a similar way, the language teacher cannot expect that the pure science (linguistics) will contain any automatic endorsement of a particular teaching procedure. Linguistics is a tool to be used by the practitioner; it can help the practitioner to operate more effectively. The teacher who is familiar with linguistics may expect to find certain teaching procedures more effective than others, but it is the teacher who must decide upon the method, and the best method is ultimately the one that is proved to be best by practical experience. Linguistics has made an impact upon language teaching in some of the following areas. In these areas, language teachers have found the use of linguistics to be particularly helpful.

1. Linguistics has generally discredited the **grammar-translation** approach, probably for two reasons:

(a) The principles on which this approach was based were found to be lacking in accuracy. The theory behind the grammar-translation approach was that **grammatical analysis** of **one** language was the prerequisite for translation into the other. Thus the analysis of *The boy sees the father* provided a grammatical framework:

Subject	*Predicate*	*Direct Object*
(noun, nominative)	(verb, present tense third person)	(noun, accusative)

This grammatical framework enabled the student to "reconstruct" the English sentence in any other language, provided he could identify the same grammatical frame: *Der Junge sieht den Vater*.

As we said before, many linguists object to this procedure on the grounds that the categories employed are not universal. "Accusative" and "nominative" are concepts that seem to fit Latin or German—highly inflected languages—better than they fit English. Linguists also believe that these allegedly universal categories really obscure the specific characteristics of the particular language. The fact that, in the example above, the German sentence could also have been *Den Vater sieht der Junge* may have been lost in the translation procedure.

(b) The other objection to grammar-translation stems from less theoretical considerations. For one thing, it is a slow procedure; it almost forces the student into establishing word-for-word correspondences or at least distorted foreign-language copies of parts of English sentences. As we have pointed out before, such equivalents, for example, *wissen/know*; *der Mann/the man*, are probably the "root of all evil." Why employ a teaching procedure that seems to reinforce the probable danger?

2. Linguists, on the other hand, generally recommend that the starting point of any exercise be a construction in the foreign language. This construction must be learned and can then be changed into other constructions by processes of transforming or expanding.

3. Linguists have also generally assumed that the processes used in linguistic analysis are useful teaching and learning procedures. Just as the linguist "finds out" that *boy* and *child* are both nouns by substituting one for the other in the same sentence, so the student finds out about grammatical categories and sentence structure by substituting words of the same category within the same sentence. The linguist "finds out" that German changes the word order if an adverb is put in the first position by comparing sentences like: *Ich tanze ≠ Heute tanze ich, Ich arbeitete ≠ Gestern arbeitete ich*. The student learns this peculiarity of German by observing it and by transforming adverb-less sentences into other sentences that have an adverb at the beginning.

4. The main stumbling block to learning a second language is the interference that comes from the first language. Through the careful comparison of the language to be learned with the native language of the learner, we can pinpoint the reasons for the difficulties experienced by the student and help him to overcome them. The reason that the speaker of English has difficulties with German modal auxiliaries (*dürfen, müssen*, etc.) lies in the fact that the usage in English (*must, may*) is in many ways different from the usage in German. Awareness of the nature of this interference can help us in giving a meaningful explanation and in constructing more helpful exercises.

5. Linguists have pointed out that language is at least primarily an audio-lingual activity and that writing is only a secondary reflection of speech. This attitude has led to the writing of grammars that are based on speech rather than writing—on the analysis of certain parts of language that are usually overlooked or only inadequately reflected in written materials (intonations, patterns, frequency of occurrence in speech rather than in written materials, etc.). The information thus furnished is of obvious use to the language teacher.

6. Linguistic analysis can help the language teacher present materials in the most efficient sequence. Since linguistic analysis clearly pinpoints the individual building stones of the languages involved, it can give valuable clues as to which stone should be put before the other, that is, which elements depend on each other, and so forth.

7. We have already made the point that linguistic analysis is based on the examination of the observable facts of language. Linguists have had, therefore, a strong kinship to so-called behavioristic schools of psychology—those schools of psychology which are based on the analysis of observable stimuli and reactions. In a sense, linguists feel that speech is "verbal behavior," observable verbal reaction to stimuli that are, at least in most cases, observable. When it comes to language teaching, linguists have, therefore, always emphasized that at least an important part of language learning consists of practice—in having the student respond to stimuli in such a fashion that the responses may be learned. Linguists are thus fairly unanimous in emphasizing that **learning about the language** is not necessarily the same activity as **learning the language**, that is, acquiring the repertory of responses which characterize a native speaker of the language.

The last category mentioned above—the relation of linguistics to language teaching—emphasizes again the point that these relationships span a wide area in which the linguist must be looked upon as having varying degrees of competence and authority. Thus the linguist (as linguist) can ultimately give little advice as to whether the so-called direct method (complete avoidance of the native language) is superior to any other. We can only point out that the avoidance of the native language is undoubtedly beneficial because it is likely to minimize interference. At the same time, the direct method is apt to depend largely on *realia*, classroom environment and activities that can be carried out within the classroom. Thus the lesson or the course is likely to be structured according to principles other than those inherent in the structure of the language.

A simple direct-method lesson may include sentences such as the following:

> *Der Professor kommt in die Klasse.*
> *Er grüsst die Studenten.*
> *Die Studenten antworten ihm.*
> *Er setzt sich, öffnet sein Buch und beginnt zu lesen.*

These sentences include a great variety of constructions, cases and genders, a reflexive verb—a mixture which shows little linguistic control. Such lack of control is perhaps not a **necessary** feature of the direct method. To the extent that it could be made compatible with attention to linguistic structure and linguistic sequencing, the direct method would certainly be endorsed by the linguist.

Finally, we should point out that some purely pedagogical devices which in the past have often been associated with linguistics and the impact of linguistics on language teaching have little relation to linguistic science and reflect at best ideas used by certain linguists in certain teaching situations. Among such devices is, for instance, that the language be first taught by a completely audio-lingual method before any reading and writing is undertaken. Although such a system reflects the linguist's emphasis on the primacy of the spoken language over writing or reading, its pedagogical efficacy must be determined in the specific learning situation by the language teacher. Similarly, the doctrine that memorization of dialogues is a most effective way of learning languages may have the endorsement of many or even most linguists; but linguistic science has nothing to offer to prove the superiority of such purely pedagogical devices. The suggestion that languages are learned best without any formal explanation of grammar may have been made by some linguists, and, indeed, all experienced language teachers and linguists will agree that the learning of grammatical rules and grammatical explanations **by themselves** will not assure adequate performance in the foreign language. Yet linguistics will not furnish evidence for the withdrawal of grammatical rules. When or whether to offer grammatical explanations is ultimately a psychological problem that must be handled in the light of psychological insight and—above all—practical experience.

CHAPTER II

Some Psychological Aspects of Language Learning

Our description of language suggests that learning a language system—native or foreign—is indeed an extremely complex task. Modern learning theory is largely based on experimentation and theories derived from extremely simplified laboratory situations (often involving animals rather than humans). To draw conclusions from those theories and apply them to the complex task of language learning is not easy and must be undertaken with care.

Perhaps one way of introducing the psychological problem of language learning is to take a model of a description of language as a starting point and to ask just what is involved in acquiring the language. Obviously the person speaking any language—foreign or native—must have acquired control of the sound system, that is, he must be able to produce the phonemes of the language and hear the contrasts between them. The morphemes and words (and their meanings) must be available to him as **responses** when they are suggested by the appropriate **stimuli**. (In other words, if, as a speaker of English, he sees a cow, this sight must, if need be, cause him to utter the word; and if the word is used, it must evoke the appropriate concept.) Yet, in addition to sounds, morphemes, and words, the learner of the language must also acquire the ability to manipulate the system as such. The native speaker learns somehow to put morphemes together according to rules, and he learns to manipulate and use the patterns of his own language. Nobody learns (even in his native language) by heart all the forms and sentences he is ever going to say. Somehow we know the patterns, we change them, we substitute one for the other and use them for our purposes. The best proof that even native-language learning involves some sort of awareness and manipulation of pattern comes from the mistakes made by children. A three-year-old may say *I *singed the song* not because he heard and learned the form **singed*, but merely because he combined (wrongly) the stem *sing* with the *-ed* ending, attributing to *sing* the same transformation pattern as to *laugh/laughed*; *kill/killed*.

Language learning—native and foreign—then involves two complex but very different tasks:

1. The acquisition of an amount of material **immediately** available to us, in other words, material that has been "memorized"—material that can be recalled and reproduced upon a specific cue. This material includes inevitably the sounds, morphemes, words, and, above all, a large number of phrases, clauses, etc., which follow the patterns of the language to be learned.

2. The acquisition of the ability to use the acquired "raw material" (a famous language teacher, Harold E. Palmer, called it "primary matter") for the purpose of converting it—transforming it—into the large number of unpredictable utterances that we shall speak or hear. Much of the pedagogical discussion and much misunderstanding is caused by language teachers stressing either the one or the other of these tasks. The fact is that both exist, that both are equally important. We must have a certain amount of raw material, "primary matter," available—and we must also be able to convert these materials into "secondary matter" —the phrases and sentences required by the specific speaking situation.

An analysis of language aptitude and language aptitude tests (see Bibliography, Carroll and Sapon) seems to bear out the statements above. The best language aptitude tests seem to be composed of sections that first of all test the prospective students' ability to hear and analyze sound contrasts. Especially in an audio-lingual course, this ability is prerequisite for easy mastery of all primary matter that is acquired through the ear. Another section of language aptitude is concerned with memory— without sound memory, the acquisition of primary matter will become too difficult. But one fact of aptitude is concerned with the ability to recognize grammatical structure, to identify whether sentences belong to the same pattern. This ability to deal with grammatical structure is no doubt the component of aptitude involved in "manufacturing secondary matter" out of the learned raw material.

The acquisition of a second language is a process similar to, but at the same time different from, the learning of the first. In the course of acquiring the first language, the amount of primary matter learned and available is, of course, extremely large. Only years of exposure to the foreign language would increase the available primary matter to an amount equal to that available in the mother tongue. Thus, in the native language, the processes involved in the manufacture of secondary matter will be less complex and less important. The sector of language experience left to secondary matter is much narrower than in the foreign language. But the foreign language has an additional tremendous disadvantage as compared to the native language. Not only is the sector left to secondary matter much larger, but the manufacturing processes used in the native language will continue to interfere.

Whatever learning theory has to offer to language teaching must be interpreted with reference to the fundamental learning tasks involved in second-language acquisition. In general, psychological theories applicable to language learning can be divided into two major types: the behavioristic type and the *Gestalt* type. The behaviorists—as the name indicates—insist that the scientific study of psychology cannot rely upon assumptions about unknown and unknowable interior processes, but must consist of the observation of overt, observable reactions (**R**) to observable stimuli (**S**). The nonbehavioristic views assert that psychological phenomena—and with them learning—involve more than overt stimulus and response. They believe that the learner brings to the learning process his own creativity, his ability to detect patterns and configurations, and his ability to recognize analogies and contrasts. Although he may indeed be influenced and shaped by outside stimuli, he also is an interacting organism, influencing the environment, and conscious of at least part of the processes in which he participates.

The behavioristic views of learning (the "**S** > **R**" school of psychology) distinguish basically between two types of learning. Both of them play a role in the acquisition of language.

The first type of learning, called **classical conditioning**, involves what is called an associational shift. This process may be described, in an oversimplified form, somewhat as follows: a piece of candy placed in the mouth serves as a stimulus (**S**) which produces salivation and a sense of pleasure as a reaction (**R**):

$$
\begin{array}{ll}
\text{candy} & > \text{pleasure} \\
\text{(physical stimulus)} & > \text{(reaction)} \\
\text{S} & > \textbf{R}
\end{array}
$$

The candy is now called by a name, "gum drop," which is repeated each time a piece of candy is presented. "Gum drop," a linguistic abstraction or symbol, is now associated with the physical object, candy, and becomes a participating or alternate factor with the original stimulus. We can denote this factor as **A**, and summarize the new situation thus:

candy	+ "gum drop"	> pleasure
(physical stimulus)	+ (name)	> (reaction)
S	+ **A**	> **R**

As a result of this association, we soon find that the word "gum drop" alone, in the absence of any actual candy, will produce salivation and what we might describe as an "echo" of sweetness and pleasure:

"gum drop"	> pleasure
(name)	> (reaction)
A	> **R**

By the association of stimulus (**S**) with a substitute or alternate (**A**), we have **conditioned** the response mechanism or reaction (**R**) so that it will function even when the associational shift from $S > R$ to $A > R$ has been completed: the organism has been conditioned to react to a symbol even when the physical stimulus is not present.

In the learning of the mother tongue, **S** corresponds to the complex of stimuli created by a situation, and **A** represents the linguistic symbols —words, forms, and structures—with which the stimuli are constantly associated. So persistent is this process of association that the linguistic symbol **A**, a substitute for reality **S**, comes to evoke whole complexes of responses or reactions **R**, and so to have **meaning**.

When the learning of a second language is undertaken, the process of associational shift cannot be repeated in this simple form. We do not refer here, however, to the simultaneous learning of two languages by a very young child in a bilingual environment, but to the acquisition of a new or foreign language by one who has already acquired the habits of his native tongue.

Much traditional methodology has focused the learner's attention on the association of elements of the new language, which we can designate as A^1, with those of the native speech, **A**. This gives us an additional substitution between **S**, the situation or external reality, and **R**, the response or meaning. Our formula would now be

$$S + A + A^1 > R$$

The meaning (**R**) of the foreign language (**A**^{1}) is thus not one derived directly from the situational association. It is also identified with the meaning of the symbols of the native language. Our formulation, therefore, may become increasingly complex. For example,

$$S + \begin{matrix} A \\ \updownarrow \\ A^1 \end{matrix} \begin{matrix} \searrow \\ \nearrow \end{matrix} R \quad \text{or} \quad A\,S + A > R \\ A^1$$

This interpolation of the native language is, of course, the reason for what we have called "interference." It leads not only to a frustrating slowdown of the process of communication but also to the intrusion of native sound and speech pattern into the second language as used by the learner.

The second basic type of learning is called **instrumental**; in addition to an association of stimulus and response, it involves also the idea of the **reward** or satisfaction which the individual receives as the result of his performance. As we watch an infant or a small puppy beginning to react to sounds and sights in his environment, it appears quite plain that responses may at first be almost completely random; but a chance few of the responses result in the satisfaction of some desire, or the lessening of an anxiety. This satisfaction or reward becomes associated with the specific response after a number of chance occurrences, and thus serves to **reinforce** the learning of a particular response in answer to a particular stimulus.

In first-language learning, the child produces sounds at random, but certain configurations of sounds will win the approval of his parents, or bring about certain results. The child is then communicating, and the reward will be his parents' attention. The response that brings reward will be learned. It is generally believed today that this process of chance and reinforcement is more fundamental in the very beginning of the infant's learning than is direct imitation of sounds and words modeled by the eager parent.

In second-language learning **conscious** imitation by the student of sounds produced by the teacher becomes an important and obvious basis for learning. Nevertheless, the value of reward or reinforcement of correct responses to speed real control seems beyond the need for argument. Our problem will be to determine what teaching or learning devices are best calculated to provide for such reinforcement by reward or approval. We must observe carefully the way we use the term "reward." A student may be anxious to get his homework done and be worried about not finishing it in time so that he can get to the baseball game. The response he produces in German, no matter how wrong, will find an immediate reward by his lessening of tension ("Thank God I'm done with the homework"), and will thus be reinforced and learned. Our goal must be to control the learning of the student in such a way that reward of any kind is reserved only for correct responses.

We should keep in mind that it is more effective to reward correct responses than to punish ("extinguish") incorrect ones, and that the reward seems more effective if it comes immediately after the response. The effectiveness of the reward as a reinforcer diminishes with every increase in delay.

In general it may be stated that language pedagogy during the past years has been more under the influence of behavioristic approaches than *Gestalt* assumptions. The reason for this is perhaps that many linguists are naturally more inclined toward behavioristic approaches: remember that we stated the linguist is primarily concerned with analyzing the **observable** verbal responses. Another reason may simply be that the behavioristic view gives us very specific help in teaching responses to specific stimuli. The notion of reinforcing responses by immediately rewarding the correct ones is of course a very fruitful one in the classroom (as well as in the language laboratory).

At the same time, however, it seems that the behavioristic view of learning is more useful in the task of what we called acquisition of primary matter than in the other essential aspect of language learning, which involves not simply acquisition of specific responses to specific stimuli but control over a system of communication. The learning of such a system evidently involves some sort of perception of the patterns used for communication—and the *Gestalt* view of learning seems more pertinent for that particular task.

Whatever view of learning we adopt, the acquisition of specific responses to specific stimuli cannot completely account for language learning. Essential to any view of language learning is, therefore, the notion of **transfer**. In other words, the responses that are learned must also be available when stimuli different from the original ones are present (otherwise the student who has learned to say *Wie geht es* in response to the stimulus *Guten Tag*, may be able to say *Wie geht es* only if he hears *Guten Tag* first). And unknown responses may have to be created according to the learner's conscious or subconscious awareness of the foreign-language pattern. In the behavioristic view the type of transfer that we have been referring to is essentially accounted for by the external situation:

a response is learned in situation A, but it can reoccur in situation B because situation B shares many elements with situation A. The non-behaviorist is more likely to stress mental processes within the learner as being responsible for the transfer (or "transposition") and is also more likely to insist that transfer is promoted through an understanding of the situation and its component elements.

There is little doubt that understanding does promote transfer. A pupil who has memorized a sentence without understanding its grammatical structure (or perhaps even without understanding the sentence) is not likely to have this sentence or a similar sentence available in response to a changed stimulus. At the same time, the necessity for understanding, the intellectual comprehension of grammar, may in some cases actually interfere with fluency in speaking and production. The language teacher here is faced with a dilemma that appears to some extent in the teaching of any complex skill. The pupil who learns to drive or to dance must get detailed instruction in the various responses involved in the performance. The exact motions of manipulating the clutch, the accelerator, the gears (or in the case of dancing, the exact sequence of steps) must be analyzed. However, the **goal** of the instruction is not the analysis, but a performance during which the pupil forgets about the analytical study. It is difficult to drive a car and at the same time to think about the operation of the clutch or the gears. It is difficult to speak a language and at the same time to think about the nominative, the accusative, or the direct object—as necessary or as helpful as these concepts may be in taking the first faltering steps in the new medium.

There are probably two ways of attacking the problem of the dancer who falters because he has to keep his mind on the sequence of the steps: (1) a great deal of practice; (2) a partner who is so interesting that he, or she, keeps his mind off the analytical process.

The same remedies apply also in the language teaching situation. The analytical awareness of grammatical patterns in no way supplants practice; sometimes it must even be counteracted by it. In addition, we can and must sometimes divert the student's attention away from the structure itself. In the initial stages of instruction this diversion may take the form of an exercise in which the student manipulates a structurally unimportant but obvious element of a grammatical construction, for example, we can—perhaps with the help of flash cards—have the student change the subject of the subordinate clause in *Ich möchte gern, dass der Lehrer nach Hause geht.* The substitution of *Professor, Onkel,* or *Tante* in this construction will divert the student's attention from the complicated structure that he is practicing. On the higher levels of instruction, the diversion process consists simply of giving the student something to talk about that is of real and genuine interest to him.

The main hindrance to language learning, however, is not the clinging to analytical understanding, but errors committed in the transfer process. At this point, let us remember again that any language response—unless it is a response which has been **specifically** learned—is the result of a transfer process. The child who uses the form *he approximated*, without having heard or learned the past tense of *approximate*, is transferring correctly, or **positively**, from his experience with forms such as *laughed* or *asked*. The child who forms the past tense **singed* or **thinked* is transferring out of the same experience—but **transferring incorrectly**. Incorrect transfers, or, as we shall call them, **negative transfers**, caused by exceptions and "breaks in consistency" in the pattern of a language, are committed quite often by the learner of a foreign language. But, as we have stated before, the learner of a second language must combat not only the "inconsistencies" of the foreign language system; he is also influenced by the transfer pattern of his own native language. If these patterns of transfer—these "manufacturing processes" of the native language—correspond with those of the foreign language, they are likely to promote **positive transfer**, that is, transfer of patterns which are correct in the foreign language; if they clash, they will lead to the transfer of incorrect patterns, that is, **negative transfer**.

A speaker of English who has learned to say *Ich bin hungrig = I am hungry* will be helped by the pattern of his native language to transfer positively to *Ich bin krank = I am sick*; *Ich bin müde = I am tired*. However, if on the basis of English transfer possibilities he manufactures *Ich bin richtig = I am right*, he has come up with a fairly nonsensical German sentence; it should have been *Ich habe recht*. In this particular case, English has been the cause of **negative transfer** (by psychological name) and **interference** (the same concept in linguistic terminology).

The primary task of foreign language teaching is, then, the maximization of positive transfer and the minimization of negative transfer. There are various strategies we can employ to minimize negative transfer.

We have already stated that avoidance of the mother tongue (direct method) is calculated to minimize negative transfer caused by interference from the native language. Another way to avoid negative transfer is simply to increase the amount of primary matter available to the individual and thus to decrease the sector of expressions in which transfer plays a role: the more practice we have in the language and the more we memorize, the fewer mistakes we are likely to commit. Here we should point out, however, that just plain memorization—although always beneficial—may also be quite uneconomical if it includes memorization of many sentences and constructions that could have been expressed by the pupil through positive transfer processes.

The early start in the foreign language is another possibility of minimizing negative transfer. Evidently in childhood the transfer processes utilized in the first language have not yet been overlearned to the extent that they will necessarily interfere with foreign language acquisition. Children can learn several languages without accent and with little or no interference of one grammatical system in the other. In addition, the early start also opens up the possibility of acquiring a larger amount of primary matter than is usually possible in a second-language curriculum. The only possible objection that could be made against the early start deals again with the economy of the process. In other words, the avoidance of **negative transfer** by the early start is most likely bought at the expense of a maximal utilization of **positive transfer**. To some extent at least the child does not transfer negatively because he cannot or does not utilize transfer to the same extent as the adult. The adult using the transfer processes of his native language is thus likely to learn the structure of the language faster than the child (but will, as the result of negative transfer, also probably make more mistakes).

With the student who has reached the age when transfer (positive and negative) is likely to be a major factor—certainly the student from junior-high-school age up—the best and most economical way of teaching is simply to concentrate explanation and practice at those points at which negative transfer is likely to occur. Therefore, a major part of this book will be devoted to the detection of these points of negative transfer and to the type of exercises that can help the student to overcome the hurdles presented by them.

CHAPTER III

Teaching Procedures

(A) THE USE OF ENGLISH IN THE GERMAN CLASS

The question of whether English should be used in a foreign language class is a vexing and important one. From the very outset of our discussion, we can point out that a good case can be made for not using it at all. The student will quite obviously not learn any German (in the sense of getting practice in listening to it and speaking it) by being exposed to English. In addition, many language teachers feel with a great deal of justification that the foreign language class should be a "linguistic and cultural island in a sea of English-speaking environment." Even the occasional use of English will detract from this concept of the language class. Finally, there is also the danger that English, if allowed into the classroom at all, may drive out the German. If we turn to English **consistently** for the purpose of explaining, assigning homework, making announcements, we keep on demonstrating to the students that whenever **real** communication is involved we can fall back on English and that the German which we and they are speaking is some sort of a game we are playing for the purpose of getting through a language course.

What, then, are the grounds on which we may justify the **occasional** use of English in our class? First of all, we may want to use English at the beginning of the course to give explanations. Explanation in German may either be incomprehensible or involve the pupil in a variety of complicated vocabulary and structures that will divert his attention from the very point we want to explain and which we want the student to practice. A brief explanation in English may save time for more concentrated learning and avoid disorganization and confusion.

Translation or explanation in English may also be the most economical way of supplying the meaning of structure and especially of vocabulary items. Here again the arbitrary avoidance of English not only makes it difficult to arrange the material according to linguistic patterns, but it may also, especially in the case of fairly obvious vocabulary items, lead to rather involved and unnecessarily lengthy explanation. It is perfectly true that building stones of different languages should not be equated. The danger involved in making these equations is likely to be greater with words like *about, when, will, shall, by*, and so on. Those little words which form or determine the over-all shape of the construction have been compared by some linguists to the mortar of the construction rather than to the stones themselves. Obviously no English explanation or translation should even be attempted for those words which have the primary purpose of denoting grammatical relationships and which we called the construction or **function words** of the language. But with words that denote obvious concepts and easily identifiable physical objects, the danger involved in giving German-English equations may not be very great. Even if the equation is not given by the teacher, it may be supplied by the student anyway. Thus, if a student meets a sentence like *Ich möchte, dass Sie das Paket sofort absenden*, and he is in doubt as to the meaning of *Paket*, it is probably better to explain that *Paket* means *package* rather than to attempt to define the word in German—a procedure which will take the student's mind off the construction he is studying, which is the real problem of the sentence above.

Other reasons for the possible use of English in a German class go beyond the realm of economy, but have an independent linguistic and pedagogical justification of their own. Difficulties usually revolve around contrasts between English and German. The use of English makes it possible to focus attention on those contrasts and drive them home to the learner. The most obvious example of the principle involved here comes from the realm of **phonology** and will be discussed with more examples and in greater detail at a later point in this book: a speaker of English will have difficulty in the pronunciation of certain German sounds because he will tend to substitute English sounds for those of German. Thus, for the vowel of German *geh* he might substitute the vowel of English *gay*. One way of combating this mistake is to contrast the English and German sounds for the student, make him conscious of the difference, teach him to identify the German and the English sounds.

This principle of overtly contrasting English and German can also be applied in the realm of **constructions**. Therefore, a drill in which the student substitutes different nouns in a construction like *Ich möchte, dass Sie den Text studieren* can be preceded by an overt comparison of that construction with the English: *I want you to study the text.* Moreover, the contrast between English and German itself can be made part of the pattern drill in which the teacher asks the student to translate sentences, such as *I want you to study the lesson*; *I want you to study the book*; *I want you to study the rule.* The student in fact goes through a pattern-drill exercise that impresses a structural difference between English and German upon his memory.

From the linguistic point of view, it is difficult to decide whether this kind of pattern drill, which consists of an overt comparison of English and German, is more useful than the exercises in which the German structure is drilled in German alone without comparison with English. The answer doubtlessly depends on psychological factors involving the student, his age, aptitude, and so on. At any rate, this kind of drill should be performed **orally**. There are at least two reasons for this. First, using the native language as an oral stimulus minimizes the danger of the student's using the English sentence as a basis for word-by-word translation. Seeing English sentences written down gives the student time to figure out correspondences between English and German building stones, the activity we have characterized as the archenemy of successful language learning. Once the overt comparison between English and German has been made, English should not be used as a basis for word-by-word translation, but only as a stimulus to provoke a German construction already known *in toto* by the student. The response triggered by the English *I want you to study this text* must be an automatic *Ich möchte, dass Sie diesen Text studieren,* and not a slow *Ich will . . . , Ich möchte, Sie . . . ,* and so forth. It is only through oral practice that we can make sure of the accuracy of the response.

The other reason for insisting on limiting oneself to the use of spoken English as the stimulus is the fact that in some cases only spoken English allows us to make an accurate comparison. Thus, the difference between *ein Deutschlehrer* and *ein deutscher Lehrer* is expressed in English by a difference in stress: *ein Deutschlehrer* is a *German⌐ teacher* (heavier stress on *German*), while *ein deutscher Lehrer* is a *German⌐ teacher* (heavier stress on *teacher*). In English we usually rely on stress, and stress alone, to emphasize a particular part of the sentence. German as a more highly inflected language can, in addition, make much greater use of word order for the same purpose. English: *Charles does not know⌐ that⌐ boy!* German: *Den⌐ Jungen kennt Karl nicht.* Such differences are often lost sight of, unless an overt comparison is made between spoken German and spoken English.

The advantage of a deliberate and limited use of English lies thus in showing the differences between English and German. Obviously this advantage is lost if we follow a practice found in some textbooks, namely that of adapting English structure to German structure to as great an extent as possible. The reason for the practice is evident. If English is used as the basis for translation into German, the manipulation of English will help the student to avoid a mistake in German in the specific sentence on which he is operating. Thus a student translating *One has told me that he is intelligent* is likely to use the correct German *Man hat mir gesagt . . .* Yet the disadvantage in always triggering German *man* by English *one* (which in the above example does not correspond to any real English usage in the first place) consists of the student not becoming fortified for the moment in which, in a real speaking situation, he will want to express his own thought of *I have been told . . .* or *They tell me that . . .*

Even if there is a choice between two equally good English constructions, one paralleling German and the other not, I should suggest that occasionally at least the construction clashing with German be made the stimulus of the pattern drill. The construction *I give Charles the book* corresponds quite neatly to the German *Ich gebe Karl das Buch*, but there is an advantage in also triggering *Ich gebe Karl das Buch* by *I give the book to Charles* in order to **avoid** the possible literal transposition of the latter sentence (. . .*zu Karl*) into German. The translation of *er hätte gehen können* by *he would have been able to go* may perhaps save the student and the teacher some trouble because both *go* and *gehen* seem to appear as infinitives. The translation *he could have gone* brings a conflict between German and English out into the open (as we shall point out again later, the English modals *can, must*, etc., unlike their German counterparts, do not form compound tenses), but the conflict must be brought out sooner or later anyway. Sweeping it under the carpet by substituting *to be able* for *can* does not solve the real problem.

What we have said really adds up to one fundamental point: the English with which German is to be contrasted must be normal English as spoken by the student. It is the student's actual behavior in English that creates the problem. For this reason the accurate and truthful description of the English as spoken by our student must be the basis of our comparison and contrast with German, since it is the way the student speaks English that creates the problem, not the way he ought to speak. To manipulate the English or to be prescriptive about it may only obscure the real point of difficulty and create unnecessary confusion. Thus the problem of having to explain to the student the different meanings of *I should work* (*Ich sollte arbeiten*; *Ich würde arbeiten*) is largely created by the idea that the student should use *I should work* as the first person of a conditional corresponding to a second person, *you would work*. The problem is created by a prescriptive assumption. Most students will naturally use *would* in the first person: *I would work* = *Ich würde arbeiten*, and *I should work* (*ought to work*) = *Ich soll*(*te*) *arbeiten*. At the same time, however, the teacher of German can hardly accept truly substandard forms of English as his point of reference, at least not without making an attempt to correct those forms. And there are also times when establishing correct English usage may be necessary for teaching correct German. For example, the confusion between *lay* and *lie* that exists in the speech of some students may have to be clarified by the German teacher in order to prevent the parallel confusion (*legen/liegen*) in German.

To sum up, the judicious use of English seems justified for a limited number of specific purposes. The main danger of using English is simply that even the occasional use may open the door to abuse. Even the suggested use in cueing for pattern drill must be put into practice quite sparingly. The author of this book once witnessed a foreign language (French) class, in which the instructor (a native speaker) used English almost throughout the class for cueing the students' answers. The result was that the pupils listened to his bad English and he listened to their bad French without providing any model for the students. Using English cueing does not correspond to a normal speaking situation, does not afford auditory practice, and must be used judiciously and sparingly in the specific situations that we have discussed.

(B) PATTERN PRACTICE

The pupil who wants to say a sentence in the foreign language has two avenues of approach to this sentence.

1. He can think of the sentence in his native language first and then fragment the sentence, unconsciously or consciously, through some sort of grammatical analysis. He can then try to put together a sentence in the foreign language by thinking first of the foreign language equivalents of the English fragments and then by trying to recombine them according to whatever rules of grammar he may remember. This process takes approximately the following form: Step 1—I want to say in German, *I do not understand you*. Step 2—*I* equals German *ich*; *do* equals German *tun*;

not equals German *nicht*; *understand* equals *verstehen*; *you* equals *du* (*dir, dich*) or *Sie* (*Ihnen*). Step 3: *do* equals *tun*, but it is not relevant since German does not use *tun* in the negative construction. *Verstehen* has to be put into the first person *Ich verstehe Sie nicht*. It is obvious that the operation we have just described is tremendously complicated and can break down at any number of points. It is nevertheless the operation that poor language learners are evidently trying to perform if they attempt to speak a foreign language. It is certainly not an operation that should be encouraged by our teaching process.

2. The operation which a good language learner performs in order to arrive at the German sentence, *Ich verstehe Sie nicht*, bypasses the fragmentation and analysis of the English sentence altogether. If he does not remember the sentence, *Ich verstehe Sie nicht*, as a unit, then the good language learner is at least likely to remember a sentence that has the same structure or a similar structure. If it is a sentence of the same structure or pattern, he can arrive at *Ich verstehe Sie nicht* by a simple process of substitution. He may remember *Ich liebe Sie nicht* or *Ich verstehe ihn nicht* and come up with the desired *Ich verstehe Sie nicht* by substituting *verstehe* or *Sie* in the original sentence. If he remembers *Ich verstehe Sie*, he must change *Ich verstehe Sie* to *Ich verstehe Sie nicht* by transforming the pattern. If the base sentence for the operation is *Ich liebe Sie*, then both a **transformation** and a **substitution** are necessary: (1) *Ich verstehe Sie* (substitution) (2) *Ich verstehe Sie nicht* (transformation). In their teaching, good language teachers therefore rely very heavily on using transformation and substitution processes and on giving the student extensive practice in using these processes. The purpose of using these processes, which are known as **pattern practice**, is:

(a) to bypass the process of using fragmentary equivalents of fragments of native utterances as bases for utterances in the foreign language.

(b) to teach the pupil through **practice and grammatical understanding** those processes which will enable him to create sentences in the foreign language.

The last point needs special emphasis because it is not always clearly understood and brought out in pedagogical discussion. The substitution and transformation exercises that form the basis of pattern practice are not designed to bypass grammar. They rely on grammatical understanding and are, in turn, supposed to reinforce it. Furthermore, pattern practice is not **primarily** a device by which the student—through repetition and minimal manipulation of a sentence—is forced to utter sentences in the foreign language. **The ultimate goal of pattern practice is to teach the student those** operations which will enable him to generate sentences in the foreign language, in other words, those grammatical procedures which allow him to convert primary matter into secondary with maximal speed and minimal interference from his native language.

The following classification of types of pattern practice is, then, primarily a model of the **grammatical procedures** the student has to learn to control and perform with considerable speed if he is to create his own German sentences from the materials and models that he has learned. Therefore, the types of pattern practice that we shall mention are essentially the **manufacturing procedures** to be taught to the student, and we shall return to them as a model for our analysis of some of the problems of German grammar. Here they are mentioned only as samples of teaching procedure, not as part of our discussion of grammatical principles.

As we have mentioned, the categories of pattern practice involve basically two broad classes: (1) those in which the pupil replaces a word in a construction by another word without changing the essential structure and (2) those which involve the change of one construction to another.

Thus one category of pattern practice involves:

1.   Substitution Procedures

This substitution can concern the major parts of speech (noun, adjective, adverb, verb) or any of the function words (conjunctions, prepositions, and so on).

Noun Substitution

TEACHER:	STUDENT*:
Ich kenne den Herrn.	*Ich kenne den Herrn.*
_____ *die Dame.*	*Ich kenne die Dame.*

If choice of article on the part of the student is desired:

TEACHER:	STUDENT:
_____ *Dame.*	*Ich kenne die Dame.*
_____ *Kind.*	*Ich kenne das Kind.*

Pronoun Replacement

Since in German the replacement of a noun by a pronoun generally does not change the basic structure of the sentence, we can include the

---

* In actual classroom practice responses may be individual as well as choral.

replacement of a noun by a pronoun (or of a pronoun by another) in the basic substitution procedure:

TEACHER:	STUDENT:
Ich kenne Karl.	*Ich kenne ihn.*
Ich kenne Maria.	*Ich kenne sie.*
Ich kenne das Buch.	*Ich kenne es.*
or:	
Ich spreche Deutsch.	*Ich spreche Deutsch.*
Er _____ .	*Er spricht Deutsch.*
Wir _____ .	*Wir sprechen Deutsch.*

Adjective Substitution

TEACHER:	STUDENT:
Ich lese das neue Buch.	*Ich lese das neue Buch.*
_____ interessant _____.	*Ich lese das interessante Buch.*
_____ schön _____.	*Ich lese das schöne Buch.*

Adverb Substitution

TEACHER:	STUDENT:
Ich lese das Buch schnell.	*Ich lese das Buch schnell.*
_____ gern.	*Ich lese das Buch gern.*
_____ langsam.	*Ich lese das Buch langsam.*

Verb Substitution

TEACHER:	STUDENT:
Ich lese das Buch.	*Ich lese das Buch.*
___ sehe _____ .	*Ich sehe das Buch.*

If choice of form is desired:

TEACHER:	STUDENT:
___ sehen _____ .	*Ich sehe das Buch.*
___ kennen _____ .	*Ich kenne das Buch.*

Verb Substitution with Morphological Change in Tense

This particular operation could also be classified as a transformation. However, since it does not change the syntactical pattern, we deal with it under the heading of substitution:

TEACHER: STUDENT:

Ich sehe das Buch.
Ich sah das Buch.
Ich lese das Buch.   *Ich las das Buch.*
Ich vergesse das Buch.   *Ich vergass das Buch.*
Ich gebe das Buch meinem Freund.   *Ich gab das Buch meinem Freund.*

Function-Word Substitution (Example: preposition)

TEACHER: STUDENT:

Ich arbeite mit meinem Freund.   *Ich arbeite mit meinem Freund.*
_____ *bei* _____ .   *Ich arbeite bei meinem Freund.*

If choice of form is desired:

TEACHER: STUDENT:

_____ *für* _____ .   *Ich arbeite für meinen Freund.*
_____ *ohne* _____ .   *Ich arbeite ohne meinen Freund.*

The other pattern-practice exercises we shall discuss involve some sort
of change in the syntactical patterns (syntactical transformation).

2. Simple Transformation Operations

The Negative Transformation

TEACHER: STUDENT:

Ich kenne diesen Mann.
Ich kenne diesen Mann nicht.
Ich gehorche diesem Mann.   *Ich gehorche diesem Mann nicht.*
Ich folge diesem Mann.   *Ich folge diesem Mann nicht.*

The Interrogative Transformation

TEACHER: STUDENT:

Karl kennt diesen Mann.
Kennt Karl diesen Mann?
Karl gehorcht diesem Mann.   *Gehorcht Karl diesem Mann?*
Karl folgt diesem Mann.   *Folgt Karl diesem Mann?*

The Passive Transformation

TEACHER: STUDENT:

Karl schliesst die Tür.

Die Tür wird von Karl geschlossen.

Karl schreibt den Brief.	*Der Brief wird von Karl geschrieben.*
Karl sucht den Schlüssel.	*Der Schlüssel wird von Karl gesucht.*

Another series of operations can be thought of as consisting of the expansion of the basic parts of speech making up the sentence. In other words, we can expand the nominal, verbal, adjectival, or adverbial part of a basic sentence.

3. Expansion Operations

Noun Expansion

The typical way of expanding the noun is, of course, by addition of a modifying adjective:

TEACHER:	STUDENT:
Ich kenne das Mädchen.	*Ich kenne das Mädchen.*
_____ *schön* _____ .	*Ich kenne das schöne Mädchen.*
_____ *hübsch*_____ .	*Ich kenne das hübsche Mädchen.*
_____ *jung* _____ .	*Ich kenne das junge Mädchen.*

Another way of expanding the noun consists of adding to the noun a genitive or a prepositional phrase:

TEACHER: *Das Buch ist interessant. Es gehört meinem Freund.*

TEACHER: *Das Buch meines Freundes ist interessant.*

TEACHER: *Das Buch ist interessant. Es gehört dem Professor.*

STUDENT: *Das Buch des Professors ist interessant.*

TEACHER: *Das Buch ist interessant. Es gehört dem Lehrer.*

STUDENT: *Das Buch des Lehrers ist interessant.*

In a very similar way a prepositional expression can be used to expand a noun.

TEACHER:	STUDENT:
Ich kenne den Mann . . . aus Wien . . .	
Ich kenne den Mann aus Wien.	
_____ *mit dem Bart.*	*Ich kenne den Mann mit dem Bart.*
_____ *aus Berlin.*	*Ich kenne den Mann aus Berlin.*

Verb Expansion

As we shall explain later, verb expansion may involve among other things the formation of a compound tense from a simple one or the inclusion of a modal auxiliary (*dürfen*, *müssen*, and so on):

TEACHER:	STUDENT:
Ich spreche mit Karl.	
Ich werde mit Karl sprechen.	
Ich arbeite mit Karl.	*Ich werde mit Karl arbeiten.*
Ich gehe mit Karl in die Stadt.	*Ich werde mit Karl in die Stadt gehen.*
Ich spreche mit Karl.	
Ich muss mit Karl sprechen.	
Ich arbeite mit Karl.	*Ich muss mit Karl arbeiten.*
Wir arbeiten mit Karl.	*Wir müssen mit Karl arbeiten.*
Du sprichst mit Karl.	*Du musst mit Karl sprechen.*

The other important way of expanding the verb is through the addition of an adverb:

TEACHER:	STUDENT:
Ich spreche mit Karl.	
Heute spreche ich mit Karl.	
Ich arbeite mit Karl.	*Heute arbeite ich mit Karl.*
Ich gehe mit Karl in die Stadt.	*Heute gehe ich mit Karl in die Stadt.*

In the above type of exercise it is also possible to keep the main sentence constant and vary the adverb:

TEACHER:	STUDENT:
Ich spreche mit Karl.	
Heute _____ .	*Heute spreche ich mit Karl.*
Jetzt _____ .	*Jetzt spreche ich mit Karl.*
Da _____ .	*Da spreche ich mit Karl.*

Adverb and Adjective Expansion

It is also possible to expand the adjectival or adverbial part of the sentence by adding other adjectives or adverbs, or by adding certain types of function words such as *sehr*, *ziemlich*, *ganz*, and so on:

TEACHER:	STUDENT:
Karl arbeitet schnell.	
_____ *sehr* _____ .	*Karl arbeitet sehr schnell.*
_____ *ziemlich* __ .	*Karl arbeitet ziemlich schnell.*
_____ *ganz* _____ .	*Karl arbeitet ganz schnell.*

Another type of transformational pattern exercise involves changing a main clause into a subordinate clause and fitting it into a sentence.

4. Subordinate Clause Operations

The subordinate clause operations may involve expansion as well as replacement and transformation. We can use them to expand the noun (in other words, add a subordinate clause to the noun), or we can use the subordinate clause to replace the noun object of a verb, or we can use it instead of an adverb.

Relative Clauses

TEACHER: *Der Mann arbeitet. Er ist glücklich. Wer ist glücklich?*

TEACHER: *Der Mann, der arbeitet, ist glücklich.*

TEACHER: *Der Schüler hat Erfolg. Er denkt viel. Wer hat Erfolg?*

STUDENT: *Der Schüler, der viel denkt, hat Erfolg.*

TEACHER: *Die Frau ist glücklich. Sie hat Kinder. Wer ist glücklich?*

STUDENT: *Die Frau, die Kinder hat, ist glücklich.*

Object Clauses

TEACHER: *Karl hat recht. Was glauben wir?*
     Wir glauben, dass Karl recht hat.

TEACHER: *Karl ist krank. Was glauben wir?*

STUDENT: *Wir glauben, dass Karl krank ist.*

TEACHER: *Hans arbeitet viel. Was glauben wir?*

STUDENT: *Wir glauben, dass Hans viel arbeitet.*

Adverbial Clauses

Use *weil* to form adverbial clauses from the second sentence:

TEACHER: *Robert arbeitet. Er will Geld verdienen. Warum arbeitet er?*

TEACHER: *Robert arbeitet, weil er Geld verdienen will.*

TEACHER: *Robert ist krank. Er arbeitet zuviel. Warum ist er krank?*

STUDENT: *Robert ist krank, weil er zuviel arbeitet.*

TEACHER: *Robert bleibt zu Hause. Er ist krank. Warum bleibt er zu Hause?*

STUDENT: *Robert bleibt zu Hause, weil er krank ist.*

TEACHER: *Robert ist unglücklich. Er muss zu Hause bleiben. Warum ist er unglücklich?*

STUDENT: *Robert ist unglücklich, weil er zu Hause bleiben muss.*

In actual practice it is possible to combine several types of pattern-practice exercises in the same operation. A favorite exercise of some teachers and in some textbooks is the **successive replacement drill:**

TEACHER:	STUDENT:
Karl arbeitete immer mit seinem Bruder.	*Karl arbeitete immer mit seinem Bruder.*
Hans _____.	*Hans arbeitete immer mit seinem Bruder.*
____ sang _____.	*Hans sang immer mit seinem Bruder.*
_____ nie_____.	*Hans sang nie mit seinem Bruder.*
_____ ohne _____.	*Hans sang nie ohne seinem Bruder.*
_____ Schwester.	*Hans sang nie ohne seine Schwester.*

Quite often a **replacement** and a **transformation** can be **combined** in the same drill. A typical example is the simple question-answer type of exercise involving replacement of nouns by pronouns; for example:

TEACHER:	STUDENT:
Haben Sie das Buch gelesen?	*Nein, wir haben es nicht gelesen.*
Haben Sie das Gedicht gelernt?	*Nein, wir haben es nicht gelernt.*
Haben Sie den Schlüssel gefunden?	*Nein, wir haben ihn nicht gefunden.*

Another apparently successful teaching device consists of utilizing visual aids (objects or pictures) for the purpose of grammatical drill.

Visual aids have always been utilized by teachers for the purpose of supplying meaning (especially in direct-method courses), but they are used most effectively to cue grammatical manipulations. Thus an object (or its picture) can supply the noun to be substituted in patterns.

Once a pattern—let us say, *Ich habe Bücher sehr gern*—has been learned, pattern practice can be cued by a picture chart containing a series of objects (or by the objects themselves), for example, apples, plums, or pears. As the teacher points to each object, the student is cued to the response: *Ich habe Äpfel sehr gern; Ich habe Pflaumen sehr gern; Ich habe Birnen sehr gern*, etc.

Another variation of pictorial cueing for pattern practice consists of the use of charts in which specific actions are depicted (for example, a man running, a child reading, a fish swimming). The specific sentences describing the actions can be cued by pointing to the pictures (*Der Mann läuft; Das Kind liest*, and so on). It is also possible to cue variations in tenses or persons. By pointing to the picture and simultaneously cueing with the word *morgen* (as agreed upon cue for the future), the teacher can elicit the response, *Morgen wird der Mann laufen*, and pointing to the next picture, *Morgen wird das Kind lesen*. Pointing to the pictures and cueing with *wir*, the teacher can elicit *wir laufen, wir lesen*, and so forth.

Perhaps the most essential aspect of pattern practice is the already mentioned fact that its ultimate goal is to teach the student the tools and operations which will lead him to self-expression. Therefore it is important that the transfer operation—in other words, the use of the pattern for expressing the student's **own** sentences—be made part of the individual pattern drill as much as possible. One way of accomplishing this goal consists of the gradual withdrawal ("fading") of the cue until the use of the pattern for self-expression is introduced. To give an example:

Step 1: Repetition

TEACHER: *Karl will, dass seine Freunde ihm helfen.*

STUDENT: *Karl will, dass seine Freunde ihm helfen.*

TEACHER: *Karl will, dass seine Eltern ihm helfen.*

STUDENT: *Karl will, dass seine Eltern ihm helfen.*

TEACHER: *Die Eltern wollen, dass Karl selbst lernt.*

STUDENT: *Die Eltern wollen, dass Karl selbst lernt.*

TEACHER: *Die Eltern wollen, dass Karl zu Hause bleibt.*

STUDENT: *Die Eltern wollen, dass Karl zu Hause bleibt.*

Step 2: Noun Substitution

TEACHER: *Karl will, dass seine Freunde ihm helfen.*

STUDENT: *Karl will, dass seine Freunde ihm helfen.*

TEACHER: ＿＿＿＿＿＿＿＿＿ *Eltern* ＿＿＿＿＿＿ .

STUDENT: *Karl will, dass seine Eltern ihm helfen.*

TEACHER: ＿＿＿＿＿＿＿＿＿ *Brüder* ＿＿＿＿＿＿ .

STUDENT: *Karl will, dass seine Brüder ihm helfen.*

Step 3: Progressive Substitution

TEACHER: *Karl will, dass seine Freunde ihm helfen.*

STUDENT: *Karl will, dass seine Freunde ihm helfen.*

TEACHER: *Der Junge* ＿＿＿＿＿＿＿＿＿＿＿＿＿ .

STUDENT: *Der Junge will, dass seine Freunde ihm helfen.*

TEACHER: ＿＿＿＿＿ *möchte* ＿＿＿＿＿＿＿＿＿＿ .

STUDENT: *Der Junge möchte, dass seine Freunde ihm helfen.*

TEACHER: ＿＿＿＿＿＿＿＿＿＿＿＿＿ *Eltern* ＿＿＿＿＿＿ .

STUDENT: *Der Junge möchte, dass seine Eltern ihm helfen.*

TEACHER: ＿＿＿＿＿＿＿＿＿＿＿＿＿＿＿＿＿ *schreiben.*

STUDENT: *Der Junge möchte, dass seine Eltern ihm schreiben.*

Step 4: Transformation

TEACHER: *Karl bleibt zu Hause. Warum?*

STUDENT: *Die Eltern wollen, dass Karl zu Hause bleibt.*

TEACHER: *Karl arbeitet schwer. Warum?*

STUDENT: *Die Eltern wollen, dass Karl schwer arbeitet.*

TEACHER: *Karl liest jetzt sehr viel. Warum?*

STUDENT: *Die Eltern wollen, dass Karl jetzt sehr viel liest.*

TEACHER: *Karl studiert fleissig. Warum?*

STUDENT: *Die Eltern wollen, dass Karl fleissig studiert.*

Step 5: Pictorial (Nonverbal) Cue—Noun Substitution

Now the teacher may use a noun chart to cue the structure and force simultaneous substitution of a noun:

TEACHER: *Ich möchte, dass der Student viel arbeitet.*

STUDENT: *Ich möchte, dass der Student viel arbeitet.*

TEACHER: (Pointing to the picture of "*der Professor*")

STUDENT: *Ich möchte, dass der Professor viel arbeitet.*

TEACHER: (Pointing to the picture of "*das Mädchen*")

STUDENT: *Ich möchte, dass das Mädchen viel arbeitet.*

Step 6: Pictorial (Nonverbal) Cue—Sentence Transformation

Now the teacher may use a chart showing performance of certain actions. The students have already learned to associate each picture with a specific basic sentence:

> *Der Student macht seine Aufgabe.*
> *Der Lehrer liest das Buch.*
> *Der Junge geht in die Schule.*

TEACHER: (Pointing to the first picture): *Ich möchte, dass der Student seine Aufgabe macht.*

TEACHER: (Pointing to the next picture)

STUDENT: *Ich möchte, dass der Lehrer das Buch liest.*

TEACHER: (Pointing to the third picture)

STUDENT: *Ich möchte, dass der Junge, in die Schule geht.*

Step 7: Situational Stimulus

Individual students should be encouraged to **use** the construction they have just learned in order to respond to a situation briefly described by one or two sentences:

TEACHER: *Warum arbeitet denn Karl immer?*

STUDENT: *Seine Eltern wollen, dass er arbeitet.*

The student may respond to a situational stimulus more remote from the original pattern:

TEACHER: *Warum weint denn der kleine Karl?*

STUDENT: (possibly, according to his ability in German or his imagination) *Seine Eltern wollen, dass er zu Hause bleibt.*

STUDENT: *Sein Bruder will nicht, dass er mit ihm ins Kino geht.*

TEACHER: *Warum bin ich schlechter Laune?*

STUDENT: (Again, all kinds of student responses are possible. Among others, I heard in actual practice:) *Der Dekan will, dass Sie zuviel unterrichten.*

STUDENT: *Ihre Frau will, dass Sie ihr zuviel Geld geben.*

The importance of the kind of practice we have just described is that it leads the student gradually from repetition to use and self-expression. It starts with repetition—in other words, an echo response in which the stimulus and response are identical. With each successive step the stimulus becomes increasingly **dissimilar** from the desired response. Transformation required that the student change the stimulus structure. In pictorial cueing the stimulus has been "faded" into a nonverbal cue and requires that the pupil perform the substitution and the transformation on a sentence which he must recall. In the final step (situational stimulus), we have finally reached the normal speaking situation. The stimulus is completely dissimilar from the expected response (the original stimulus has been "faded" completely), for example, *Warum weint denn der kleine Karl?* The **response** must now be available as part of the student's **active repertory** for **self-expression and communication**.

Another simple device, designed to make pattern manipulation into a creative activity on the part of the student, consists in employing exercises of progressive substitution, telling the student to make sentences (of his own choice) by substitution for the different parts of speech in a specific sentence. The teacher assigns only the basic sentence, such as *Wenn ich viel Geld hätte, würde ich nach Deutschland fahren.* The students make up their own sentences by providing **their own** substitutions (*Wenn ich viel Geld hätte . . . , Wenn ich viel Zeit hätte . . . , würde ich nach Rom fahren; . . . nach Rom fliegen,* and so on).

In a similar way to the one above, we can designate a specific transformation or series of transformations as a special exercise. For instance, Exercise A consists of performing the negative, passive, and interrogative transformations in a sentence. Depending on the type of practice desired, it would be understood that these operations are to be performed on the same basic sentence or that they are to be successive operations performed on the product of the preceding operation. Thus the teacher assigns the sentence *Robert macht die Reise nach Wien,* and the student responds (in spoken or in written form) with *Robert macht die Reise nach Wien nicht. Die Reise nach Wien wird von Robert gemacht. Macht Robert die Reise nach Wien?* In the successive chain variation of this type of exercise, the student's response would be, *Robert macht die Reise nach Wien nicht. Die Reise nach Wien wird von Robert nicht gemacht. Wird die Reise nach Wien von Robert nicht gemacht?*

So far we have stressed the importance of pattern practice as part of the student's training in speaking and self-expression. However, language learning is also concerned with the development of the **passive** skills of comprehension of speech and reading. It is especially in connection with the latter that we must pay special attention to the patterning of language and to developing the students' ability to grasp the patterns of the written page as quickly as possible. Much of the pedagogical discussion of recent years seems to have assumed that reading ability is a secondary development which follows more or less automatically if speaking fluency is developed. It is probably true that an initial audio-lingual attack on a language will facilitate and increase reading speed. At the same time, there is the danger that the automatic nature of the development of reading skills may be taken for granted. No such automatism exists. Every speaker has a more or less complete audio-lingual control of his native language— which does not prevent countless native speakers of English from being slow readers, "reading failures," or in need of remedial reading courses. In addition, we must remember that in most languages the basic structures do not appear in the same form in writing and reading and in the audio-lingual realm. The degree of difference varies from language to language. In German, in any case, the difference is quite considerable, indeed.

To listen to speech signals in the medium of sequence in time, to use them in that medium, and to recognize quickly their written counterparts in the medium of space (on the printed page) are by no means identical processes. The second process must be the object of specific training. Good readers have evidently the ability to recognize quickly the structural signals of the sentences they are facing. This ability to see the structural signals and grasp the grammatical meaning of the sentence first enables them to infer in many instances the meaning of lexical items from the grammatical meaning and from the context. The poor reader (just like the poor speaker) deals with fragments—individual words—without recognizing the pattern as a whole. He must be trained to look for the **structural signals**.

The teaching of reading, therefore, takes the form of teaching the visual recognition of patterns. This can be done by underlining the structurally significant elements of the sentence, for example, *Das meinem Freunde nicht bekannte Buch wurde von ihm doch besprochen*. Another device that focuses the student's attention on the structurally important signals is a type of pattern practice in which the items conveying the grammatical meaning (and perhaps some skeletal lexical meaning) of the sentence are given on the printed page. Parts of the structure—those that contain slots for lexical items which could be inferred from context—are left blank, for example, *Ich lese das____das mein____mir____gegeben hat*. The student is then asked to provide a meaningful completion of the sentence. This procedure trains the student in sorting lexical items from structure and in making the kind of contextual inferences necessary to the rapid reading process.

(C) THE LANGUAGE LABORATORY

In many teaching situations the pattern-practice type of exercise discussed in the preceding section has been primarily relegated to the language laboratory. A few words concerning the language laboratory and its uses may therefore be in order. There is no need to duplicate here the description of laboratories or laboratory techniques found in several recent and excellent publications. Nor is there any need to underline the potential usefulness of the laboratory as such. A few salient facts, however, should be recalled.

First of all, there are different types of laboratories. Some provide only for listening on the part of the student. Others provide for the possibility of the student responding (and hearing his responses through the earphones). The most advanced kind of laboratory affords the student the possibility of recording his responses so that they may be available for his or the teacher's or joint inspection. But perhaps even more important than the facilities of the laboratory are the uses to which it is put. Here we must distinguish between two very different situations: (1) the laboratory provides flexibility according to individual student need; (2) the laboratory provides no such flexibility and is utilized instead of a block of time available for classroom instruction. There is little doubt that the **major** contribution of the laboratory is realized only in situation 1, achievement of flexibility according to individual need and aptitude. This flexibility can be brought about in two very different ways. One consists of giving the student flexible access to the laboratory. The good student (or less motivated student) may use it for only a short time. The less capable student (or highly motivated student) has the opportunity to increase his contact with the language to whatever level he desires. This type of flexibility exists in many of the library-type laboratories, especially on the college level. The other type of flexibility is brought about by allowing the student to proceed at his own rate of speed. This necessitates a complete reorganization of the language course and the use of so-called programed materials—teaching materials that can be used for the purpose of self-instruction.

If the laboratory is used simply to replace classroom instruction, it can, of course, still provide certain advantages. It can provide welcome relief for a tired teacher who can relegate the more mechanical aspects of pattern practice (repetition, substitution) to the laboratory. It can give the pupil exposure to a variety of correct models. In the classroom the pupil can give only a limited number of individual responses per class hour. In the laboratory the number of individual responses can be increased tremendously. The tape can provide immediate confirmation (and thus reinforcement) of every correct response. What should be kept in mind, however, is that these advantages of the laboratory depend on the assumption that the pupil actually goes through the drills and exercises provided on the tape. If he sits in front of the microphone silently with his mind wandering away from the business of language learning, the advantage of the laboratory will remain questionable.

It is thus essential in any kind of laboratory work that the pupil's attention remain focused on his task. The good language teacher must learn to keep the pupil's attention on the lab work by providing "intrinsic" or at least "extrinsic" motivation for the lab performance. By intrinsic motivation we mean providing material that is of sufficient interest to the pupil to capture his attention. By extrinsic motivation we understand that the pupil's attention is somehow forced on the laboratory task: the tape provides material not otherwise available; the student knows that his performance is being monitored; the lab session ends with a very short quiz dealing with the material covered during the session.

In conclusion we should emphasize again that the main potential of the laboratory consists of providing flexibility. Since generally flexibility of instruction is a goal toward which education is moving, we can assume that increasing attention will be given to the development and the use of programed materials for laboratory instruction. In programed materials the course is divided into individual learning steps. These steps are small-sized, so that a correct response by the student is likely. If he responds correctly, the answer is confirmed and he is allowed to go on to the next step. An incorrect response may force him to go through different versions of the same exercises or to take the same step over gain. The control over the "shaping" of the students' behavior that programing affords promises a great deal in increasing their success and in reaching pupils who otherwise have not been able to become successful language learners. At the same time, however, many features of programing—such as the optimal size of the learning step—remain problematic, and programs devised so far seem to have been more successful in insuring the students' learning of primary matter (in the programer's language a **specific**, or **formal**, repertory of responses) than in bringing about the even more essential transfer skills (a repertory of **thematic** responses).

PART TWO

CHAPTER IV

General Phonetics and Phonemics

(A) PHONETICS

The raw material of language consists of sounds. The science concerned with the study of speech sounds is **phonetics**. Phonetics can approach the study of speech sounds from two very different points of view: it can study the properties of the sounds themselves—that is, the exact nature of the sound waves as they progress through the air; or it can study the way in which the sounds are produced by the human speech organs. The branch of phonetics that studies the sounds themselves is called **acoustic phonetics**, and the study of the sound production is called **articulatory phonetics**. Acoustic phonetics has made important strides during the past years as the result of the discovery and perfection of machines that allow us to analyze the speech sounds in great detail. But from the viewpoint of the language teacher, articulatory phonetics will continue to be the more important branch of phonetics.

There are several good textbooks in existence, all dealing in great detail with the science of articulatory phonetics. In this chapter we shall, therefore, summarize and review the most important concepts of phonetics that are useful to the teacher of German, rather than try to give a detailed account of the discipline.

Phoneticians have for some time been concerned with the creation of a phonetic alphabet. They have worked out and are still perfecting an **international phonetic alphabet**. Ideally, such an alphabet would have one symbol, and one symbol only, to identify without ambiguity any speech sound possible in any of the languages existing today. In presenting the résumé of phonetics, we shall emphasize only those sounds and symbols which are of importance for the teacher of German. We shall follow the customary procedure of presenting phonetic transcriptions within square brackets: [ ].

Speech sounds are traditionally classified as vowels and consonants. In the production of vowels, the air stream passes through the larynx over the vocal cords, and their vibration creates sounds that are modified in the oral cavity by the other speech organs. At no time during the production of the sound is the air stream interrupted or impeded. In the production of the consonants, however, while passing through the speech organs, the air stream meets a definite obstacle that impedes or momentarily stops the sound.

Turning our attention first to the classification of consonants, we find that there are three possible criteria according to which they can be described. The first classification considers the already mentioned activity of the vocal cords. The actual mechanism that correlates the vibration of the vocal cords and the production of a consonant is quite complicated. But in somewhat simplified fashion we may say that we call a consonant **voiced** if the vocal cords vibrate throughout the production of sound, whereas we consider a consonant as **unvoiced** if throughout most or all of the production of the sound the vibration of the vocal cords is absent. On that basis we call the initial sound of English *bin* voiced, while that of *pin* is unvoiced; the initial sound of English *father* is unvoiced, and that of *veal* is voiced.

The second criterion for the classification of consonants considers the **manner of production**. We have already mentioned that in the production of consonants the air stream meets an obstacle. If during the production of the sound the air stream is actually completely interrupted, we call the sound a **stop**. A stop, then, is a sound that is produced by the act of closing and opening the path taken by the air during sound production. In this process of opening and closing, the air is often allowed to build up pressure against the obstacle and is then permitted to escape suddenly when the obstacle is removed. Stop sounds are also frequently referred to as **plosives**. The initial sounds of the English *pick*, *tin*, *can*, and *get*, etc., are all plosive or stop sounds.

All sounds produced without any complete stoppage of the air stream are called **continuants** (vowels too are, therefore, continuants in the strict sense). Among the consonants we can distinguish different types of continuants. One important type is the **fricative**. In the production of the fricative, the air stream meets an obstacle; there is no complete closure, but rather a constriction of the speech organs, and throughout the production of the sounds the air is allowed to pass through the constriction. The initial sounds of the English *father*, *veal*, *thin*, *this*, *sin*, and *ship* are all fricative sounds, produced with air friction as they pass through a constriction of the vocal apparatus.

In the case of another group of consonants, there is no real narrow constriction of the speech organs, but a modification or narrowing of the speech tract at one point or another during the production of the sound. These consonants are called **resonants**, and the initial sounds of the English *man*, *news*, *lion*, *ran*, *water* are examples of the resonants. In the case of the initial sounds in *man*, *neat*, or the final sound in *song*, the passage through the mouth is closed, but the passage through the nose is opened. It is for this reason that these resonants are also called **nasals**. In the case of [l], as in *lion*, the aperture is also closed by the contact that the tongue makes against the upper gum, although the air is allowed to escape freely at both sides of the tongue. The resonants produced in such a manner are called **laterals**. From the way we have characterized resonant consonants (absence or presence of any stoppage or even real constriction), it is also quite clear that in fact there is little absolute difference in kind between resonant consonants and vowels. As a matter of fact, vowels may be classified as resonants and the distinction between vowel and consonant—sharp and obvious if we compare vowels with stops or even fricatives—becomes blurred in the case of the resonant sounds and is difficult to make with any real precision. From the strictly phonetic point of view, it is therefore a fairly arbitrary distinction.

Before leaving the discussion of the manner of production, one more type of sound must be introduced: when producing a stop sound like the [t] in *tin*, the air stream is released suddenly after a brief stoppage. When, on the other hand, the obstacle is removed quite slowly, the air, instead of escaping with the explosion of the plosive, is allowed to pass over the obstacle more gradually. The result is that a fricative type of sound is produced. Instead of [t] as in *tin*, we get a sound that resembles [t] followed by [ʃ] as, for instance, in *chin*. This kind of sound, a stop with a slow release, is called an **affricate**.

The next comment concerns the sound [s] itself: how does it, for instance, differ from the initial sound of *thin* [θ] with which so many speakers of German are apt to confuse it? For one thing, [s] is produced with the tip of the tongue in a different position than in the case of [θ]. This is not the main difference, however. Both [s] and [θ] are fricative sounds. This means that the air is creating friction as it passes through a narrow opening, but the shape of the opening is different for the two sounds; for [θ] (just as, for instance, for [f] and [v]) the opening is wide from side to side and narrow from top to bottom. Such sounds are called **slit-fricatives**. For [s] the opening is narrow from side to side and deep from top to bottom. The tongue is slightly grooved by a raising of the edges: [s] is called a **groove fricative**. The consonant sounds corresponding to the boldface letters in *pleasure* [ʒ] or *shine* [ʃ] or *rose* [z] are all groove fricatives. Since the grooved kind of opening results in those sounds having a hissing quality, they are also frequently called **sibilants**.

As far as the manner of articulation is concerned, two more types must be considered: the **trill** or **vibrant**, and the **flap**. The latter is produced by a single rapid movement of an articulator. It may be compared to a very short stop sound: the sound which in the speech of many Americans corresponds to the [tt] of *butter* is such a flap sound. For the student of German, however, the trill or vibrant category is more important. A vibrant consists of the very rapid alternation of sounds produced by the vibration of a flexible speech organ. The "official" standard /r/ of the German *"Bühnenaussprache" is produced by a vibration* of the tip of the tongue. The much more common German /R/ (heard in most parts of Germany) is produced by a vibration of the uvula.

The third criterion in consonant classification concerns the place of stoppage of the air stream, or of maximum constriction of the speech organs: the **point of articulation**. The main classification proceeds according to the lower articulator used in the production of the sound, the lower of the speech organs which produce the stoppage or constriction. If this organ is the lower lip, we call the sound **labial**; if it is the tip of the tongue (the apex), the sound is called **apical**; if it is the front of the tongue, the sound is a **frontal**; if it is the back of the tongue (the dorsum), the sound is called **dorsal**. Thus, the initial sound of *pin* is a labial, that of *tin* is an apical, that of *chin* is a frontal, and that of *kin* is classified as a dorsal. For most purposes this general classification according to the lower articulator is not precise enough. Therefore the usual classification considers the lower as well as the upper articulator. The following table summarizes the more precise classification according to both articulators involved:

Upper Articulator	Lower Articulator	Name of Sound
upper lip	lower lip	bilabial
upper teeth	lower lip	labio-dental
teeth	tip of tongue	dental
gums of upper teeth (alveolae)	tip of tongue	alveolar
palate	tip of tongue (curled back against the palate)	retroflex
gums of upper teeth (alveolae)	front of tongue	alveo-palatal
front of palate	front of tongue	prepalatal
back of palate	back of tongue	palatal
velum (soft palate)	back of tongue	velar
uvula (back of velum)	back of tongue	uvular

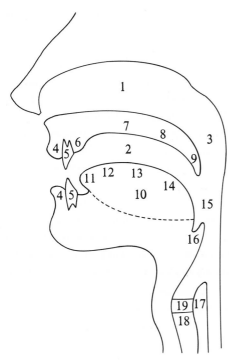

1. Nasal Cavity
2. Oral Cavity
3. Nasal passage
4. Lips
5. Teeth
6. Alveole
7. Hard Palate
8. Soft Palate
9. Uvula
10. Tongue
11. Tip of Tongue
12. Front of Tongue
13. Middle of Tongue
14. Back of Tongue
15. Pharynx
16. Epiglottis
17. Glottis
18. Larynx
19. Vocal Cords

Most of these points of articulation can be easily demonstrated by English sounds. Initial sounds of the following words may serve as illustration. Note how the point of articulation shifts back as you say the following:

1. **p**in   (4, 4)*
2. **f**in   (5, 4)
3. **th**in   (5, 11)
4. **t**in   (6, 11)
5. **r**ed   (6–7, 11)
6. **ch**in   (6–7, 12)
7. **y**et   (7, 12)
8. **k**in   (7, 12–13)
9. **c**ot   (8, 14)
10. German: *R*ache (9)

It is, of course, possible to produce sounds that have their point of articulation even farther back than the uvula, namely, in the larynx. Thus we can produce a stop just by the closure and opening of the vocal cords. This sound, a glottal stop (symbol: ʔ), is produced in some languages (in German, and, to a somewhat lesser degree, in English) before any word beginning with a vowel sound. Some speakers of English, especially along the Eastern Seaboard such as New York and New Jersey, say a glottal stop in a word like *bottle* [baʔl]. **A fricative glottal sound** is produced if the air stream is allowed to pass through the constriction created between the vocal cords without any further modification taking place in the rest of the speech tract: the [h] sound of *have* and *her* is such a **glottal fricative**.

Before summarizing our discussion of consonants, brief mention must be made of concomitant or secondary features: certain types of articulation that may accompany the articulation of a consonant. Thus the raising of the middle of the tongue against the palate may accompany the articulation of a consonant, which is then "palatalized." Or a rounding of the lips may take place while a dental or velar stop is pronounced, thus "labializing" that stop, for instance, the initial sound of English *quick* (kwɪk) can be interpreted as a **labialized stop**. The "aspiration" of a stop may also be an important accompanying feature: if after the release of a stop, air pressure is allowed to build up immediately (and before the production of the following vowel), a glottal fricative [h] will be heard between the stop and that vowel. This is the case in languages such as English or German in which most word initial stops are aspirated. On

---

* The first number refers to the upper articulator, the second number to the lower articulator (see p. 53).

the other hand, if after the stop the buildup of air pressure is delayed until the production of the following vowel, the stop will be unaspirated (as in French and the other Romance languages).

What we have reviewed here may seem a rather formidable array of terminology. There is no need for the student ever to hear it. The teacher, on the other hand, may find it quite useful to know the terminology of phonetics. Some control of this nomenclature is needed to follow pedagogically important discussion in professional journals; even more important, the control of the nomenclature implies a basic understanding of how sounds are produced. There is obviously no point in memorizing that "the English /t/ is an alveolar unvoiced stop." The real point is that for the one who understands the nomenclature, it gives in precise fashion the information about the pronunciation of the English /t/. Once that person knows how the English /t/ is pronounced, he has no need to memorize the nomenclature, which is actually nothing but a condensed description of the pronunciation of the sound.

With this in mind let us review with the help of the table on page 56 the terminology we have learned so far. In it the points of articulation are given at the left in such a way that we move from the lips back as we proceed down the table. The manners of articulation are distinguished at the top of the table, and so is the contrast of voiced vs. unvoiced. Examples are taken from English with written symbols representing the sounds marked in boldface.

We have already stated that the transition from consonant to vowel is really a gradual one. There is a group of sounds which are borderline cases and which are, therefore, classified as either **semiconsonants** or **semivowels**. For instance, the initial sound of the English *water* /w/ is a **labial semivowel**, produced with a rounding of the lips. The initial sound of the English *yes* /j/, in which the maximum construction occurs between the front of the tongue and the gums, is classified as an **alveopalatal semivowel**. English /r/ as in *red*, for which the tip of the tongue is curled back and raised against the gums or palate may be classified as an **alveolar**, or **retroflex**, **semivowel**. Since vowels are voiced and produced without any obstacle to the air stream, we must classify them according to a method different from the one used for the consonants. Again, however, we can use different categories or points of reference. One of the most important points of reference used for classification of the vowels is the **position of the tongue**. When we say the vowel of German *sie*, the front part of the tongue is raised up high and pushed forward in the oral cavity. If we say the vowel of German *du*, the back of the tongue is raised high in the oral

Manner Points	STOPS		AFFRICATES		FRICATIVES				RESONANTS	
					slit		*groove*		*lateral*	*nasal*
	voiced	*unvoiced*	*voiced*	*unvoiced*	*voiced*	*unvoiced*	*voiced*	*unvoiced*		
Bilabial	b (**bin**)	p (**pin**)								m (**man**)
Labio- dental					v (**vat**)	f (**fat**)				
Dental					ð (**then**)	θ (**thin**)				
Alveolar	d (**din**)	t (**tin**)					z (**zinc**)	s (**sink**)	l (**late**)	n (**no**)
Alveo- palatal			ǰ (**gin**)	č (**chin**)			ʒ (**vision**)	ʃ (**nation**)		
Velar	g (**goat**)	k (**coat**)								ŋ (**sing**)
Glottal								h (**hat**)		

cavity and pushed far backward. If we say the vowel of German *da*, the tongue is generally between the forward and back position in a central location—but rather low in the oral cavity.

According to the position of the tongue during the production of the sound, the phonetician can now classify the vowels into **front vowels**, **central vowels**, and **back vowels** (depending on whether the highest part of the tongue is toward the front, center, or back of the oral cavity) and into **high**, **mid**, and **low vowels** (depending on the position of the tongue in the vertical dimension of the oral cavity).

In other words, the classification can be used to establish nine compartments within the oral cavity. According to the tongue position during the production of the vowel, the letter may then be classified as high front, mid front, low front, high central, and so on. Within each compartment, further tongue positions may be specified. Vowels produced within each compartment can be subdivided into close, neutral, and open, according to the position of the tongue along the vertical axis. Vowels can be classified as more or less central according to the horizontal axis.

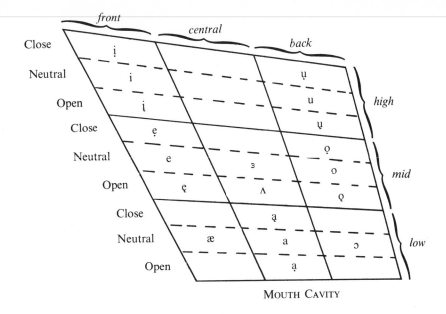

MOUTH CAVITY

The following are some examples of vowel sounds classified according to the scheme above.

High front vowels	close	[i̦]	German	*sie*
	central	[i]	English	*beat*
	open	[i̦]	English	*bit*
Mid front vowels	close	[e̦]	German	*See*
	neutral	[e]	English	*gay*
	open	[e̦]	English	*get*
Low front vowels	neutral	[æ]	English	*fat*
Mid central vowels	neutral	[ɜ]	English	*shirt*
	open	[ʌ]	English	*but*
Low central vowels	close	[a̦]	German	*satt*
	neutral	[a]	English	*car*
	open	[a̦]	German	*saht*
High back vowels	close	[u̦]	German	*du*
	neutral	[u]	English	*food*
	open	[u̦]	English	*foot*
Mid back vowels	close	[o̦]	German	*wohl*
	neutral	[o]	English	*bone*
	open	[o̦]	German	*Wolle*
Low back vowels	neutral	[ɔ]	English	*fought*

Aside from the position of the tongue, the pronunciation of the vowel is also influenced by the lip position. With the examples of vowels given so far, we have taken for granted that all front vowels are produced with the lips widely spread (watch the position of the lips in German *sie*, English *beat*) and all the back vowels are produced with the lips rounded (watch the position of the lips in the production of the vowels of German *du*, English *food*). There is, of course, no reason why these conditions of lip-rounding cannot be reversed. This reversal is often somewhat difficult for the speaker of English, but unrounded back vowels and rounded front vowels are common in many languages. At any rate, rounded front vowels exist in German:

Rounded high front vowels

| | close | [ü̦] | German | *Hüter* |
| | open | [ü̦] | German | *Hütte* |

Rounded mid front vowels

| | close | [ö̦] | German | *Höhle* |
| | open | [ö̦] | German | *Hölle* |

In addition to tongue position and lip action, several other features can help us to distinguish vowels. Some vowels are produced with more muscular energy than others. We refer to such vowels as **tense** vowels, and we consider vowels produced with less muscular energy as **lax**. German or French vowels are generally tenser than the vowels of English. The stressed vowels of German *Mut* and *Sohle* are tenser than the stressed vowels of *Mutter* or *sollen*.

If during the production of a vowel sound the velum is flapped down so that part of the air stream can escape through the nose, then the vowel is **nasalized**. If the velum closes the nasal passage, the vowel is strictly **oral**. In French the distinction between **nasal** and **oral** vowels is a very important (phonemic) one. In German and English, nasality of the vowel has no such important function and occurs only in the neighborhood of nasal consonants.

Vowels can also be classified according to their **duration**. Since all vowels are, of course, continuants, their pronunciation can vary considerably in length. The vowel sound of *sea* is normally shorter than that of *seed;* the vowel of German *bitte* is shorter than the vowel of *bieten*. It is also possible that the pronunciation of the vowel may change considerably during its production, especially with long vowels. We may start the pronunciation with one tongue position and end up with a different one, or the lip position may change during the pronunciation of the vowel. If the changes occurring during the pronunciation of the sound are indeed considerable, we may think of the sound being a combination of two vowels, a **diphthong**; if there are no or only very small changes taking place during the production of the sound, we interpret the vowel as a single unit or a **monophthong**. Thus English [ai] in *buy* is certainly a diphthong, German [i̯] in *bieten* is a monophthong.

(B) PHONEMICS

Before turning to the comparison of the German and English sound systems, we should emphasize once more the difference between the **phonetic** and **phonemic** approaches, which we referred to at the very beginning of this book. A famous linguist once said that the only really accurate **phonetic** record or transcription of speech is a high-fidelity recording. If we wanted to be phonetically accurate, we would have to transcribe every variation, every individual peculiarity. In the preceding discussion of phonetic characteristics, we noted that in phonetics we are often dealing with a continuum without a dividing line. At what point can we say that there is enough variation within the pronunciation of a vowel so that we must call it a diphthong rather than a monophthong? How long must a vowel be so that we can say it is long and not short—or medium long? The answer to all of these questions is, of course, that we ultimately decide these questions from the point of view of significance within a specific language system; in other words, from the **phonemic** point of view. The vowel of English *sea* [i] is normally longer and more diphthongal than the vowel of *leave*, which in turn is generally pronounced longer and with more diphthongization than the vowel of *beat*. This is part of an English speech habit to pronounce final stressed vowels longer than vowels that are followed by consonants; and to pronounce vowels before voiced consonants somewhat longer than vowels before unvoiced consonants. Most speakers of English are not particularly aware of this distinction. It is a more or less predictable variation. In a **phonemic** transcription in which we use the same symbol for the different variants (allophones) of the same phoneme, *bee, leave, beat*, would be transcribed with the same vowel symbol /bi/, /liv/, /bit/. In a **phonetic** transcription we would have to attempt to take cognizance of the variation, perhaps transcribe [bi:], [li.v], [bit].

A phonemic transcription, then, uses the same symbol for all the possible variants of the same phoneme. Yet another characteristic of a phonemic transcription, which should be understood by the teacher, consists of the fact that it constitutes a linguist's **interpretation** of the phonetic facts, rather than the phonetic facts themselves. Just because two linguists may transcribe the same word differently does not mean that one of them must be "wrong," nor that they are dealing with different facts. The vowels of English *beat* and *bit*, and the vowels of English *food* and *good* are obviously different. The vowel of *beat* is higher than the one of *bit*, so is the vowel of *food* higher than the one of *good*. The vowels of *beat* and *food* are also more diphthongal and longer than the vowels of *bit* and *good*. In the phonemic interpretation we can pin the title of **phonemic** difference on any one of these distinctions. If we emphasize the difference in height of the tongue as the significant one, we consider the difference of the vowels of *beat* / *bit*; *food* / *good*, as a difference between two phonemes: /bit/ /bịt/; /fud/ /gụd/. If we interpret the difference as being due to the distinction diphthong and monophthong, we can come to the conclusion that the vowel of *food* is really the one of *good* followed by an upglide and lip-rounding, whereas the vowel of *beat* is really the one of *bit*, followed by an upglide: /bijt $\neq$ bit/; /fuwd $\neq$ gud/; and if we interpret the difference as one of length alone, then our transcription becomes /fu:d $\neq$ gud/; /bi:t $\neq$ bit/ (: being the symbol for phonemic length).

Similar cases in which differences of interpretation can lead to differences in phonemic transciption can also occur with consonants. Thus we have stated in the discussion of phonetics that some stops are produced with slow release. The result is a stop really followed by a continuant produced at the same point of articulation: an affricate as in English *chin*, or German *zu* (phonetically [*tsu*]). The question arises, then, should such an affricate be interpreted as **one** phoneme or as **two**? The answer is that linguists will and can interpret either way—usually according to what makes more sense within a given language system. Therefore, for reasons which are of no immediate interest here, the affricate of English *chin* is usually interpreted as one phoneme, /čin/, whereas the one of *zu* is interpreted as t + s (*zu* = /*tsu*/).

The teacher should never confuse the phonemic transcription (or the phonetic one) with the reality for which it stands. The advantage of phonemic interpretation and transcription, if properly understood, consists in giving us a systematic understanding of the sounds—and differences between sounds—with which a language operates. We know that our student must be able to hear and produce the phonemic differences of German, or he will never be able to understand or communicate. The phonemic analysis of German and English will show us clearly which phonemes of German will be difficult for American students and which must be emphasized in our teaching.

CHAPTER V

Teaching Pronunciation

(A) GENERAL PROBLEMS

In the teaching of pronunciation and the correction of pronunciation mistakes, it is important to distinguish the different types of pronunciation problems that might arise:

1. The most important and most obvious one occurs if the foreign language utilizes a sound that has no counterpart at all in the native language. The sounds corresponding to German *ch*, *ü*, *ö*, for instance, are cases in point. If the student is not able to imitate these sounds correctly, he needs to be told exactly how to produce them. These completely new sounds pose a problem, yet quite often they do not turn out to be the most persistent pronunciation problem.

2. Another source of mispronunciation arises when the native language has a sound that is an approximation of a sound of the foreign language. In such cases the pupil is likely to substitute the native sound for the foreign one; for example, English /l/ for German /l/, English /e/ for German /ẹ/. This kind of substitution is not likely to lead to serious misunderstanding, but it turns out to be the most persistent and often obnoxious mark of the foreign accent. In order to pronounce the foreign sound correctly, the student may not only need instruction in how to say it, but may also have to receive detailed training in discrimination between the German sound and the English sound which he is substituting. Unless such training is received early in the course, the student may simply continue to substitute the English sound for the German one, and thus get cumulative practice in doing the wrong thing. Continued exposure to

the foreign language does **not** necessarily correct this kind of substitution error. We all are familiar with people who may live in a country for years and acquire fluency in the language but who **show hardly any improvement** in their accuracy of pronunciation.

3. A third kind of problem may arise if a sound which exists in the native language is used differently within the foreign language system. Theoretically this problem should not be a major one, although at times it turns out so. The native language may use a phoneme in only one specific position, and transposing it into another position may be difficult. If we tried to say a word that begins with the phoneme /ŋ/ (sing = siŋ), we may have great difficulty pronouncing the sound. (Fortunately we need not face this problem in teaching German.) Often the native language may possess the foreign sound, but only as a variant—an allophone in a specific position. Transposing this allophone into a different environment may be a problem.

4. An important set of problems can be created by orthography—the sound-symbol relationship of the foreign language. If the sound-symbol relationship of a language is irregular, then the language is often classified as "difficult to pronounce." In a sense, this is also often a misstatement. Whether a language is difficult to pronounce depends primarily on how many new phonemes it contains for the person learning it as a second language (no language seems difficult to pronounce for a native). At the same time, however, it is perfectly obvious that a complicated sound-symbol relationship can create problems. If the pupil learns to associate one symbol, such as *ei* in *receive*, with a particular sound, namely, /i/, and then uses this knowledge to pronounce from the printed or written page a word in which this relationship no longer holds true, as in English *rein*, he will obviously make a mistake. Fortunately the sound-symbol relationships of German are more constant than those of English so that the errors which the student may make by wrongly extending German sound-symbol relations are not numerous. As a matter of fact, the wrong extension into German of sound-symbol relationship learned for English seems to be a somewhat larger problem, for example, extension of the equation *ei* = /i/, as in *receive*, to German *mein*.

As far as the fight against orthographically caused mispronunciation is concerned, two main avenues of attack are open to the language teacher. One avenue consists of withholding orthography and attacking all new materials audio-lingually in order to achieve correct pronunciation **before** the pupil sees the printed word. The other avenue is to give a great deal of reading (aloud) and writing (dictation) practice at just those points at which the orthographically caused error occurs. For example, the pupil who pronounces *sein* as [sin] is asked to read aloud and write upon dictation a series of words like *dein, sein, Wein, fein, klein*, and so on.

These two avenues need not be mutually exclusive. A teacher of German may attempt to avoid spelling pronunciation first by an audio-lingual approach, then use the intensive sound-symbol practice at a later stage in the course, or with those students who develop orthographically caused mispronunciations in spite of the initial audio-lingual attack.

5. Perhaps a final category of mispronunciations exists when orthography and genuine pronunciation problems combine to create a problem for the student. The case of the German /r/ may be given as an example. It is first of all a pronunciation problem—it is not at all like the English /r/ (a retroflex semivowel), but a trill (usually produced with the uvula). Yet the fact that both English and German use—unfortunately—the same orthographic symbol for the sound will make the substitution of the English sound for the German even more likely. In addition, the German /r/ in final position, as in *sehr, der*, is very different from the /r/ in initial position, as in *Rache, richtig*. It is not a trill but really a vowel (central to back, with unrounded lips: [ʌ]). The student may, as a result of the identity in orthography, substitute either the English /r/ or the German initial [R] (trill with the uvula). The latter substitution is not as bad as the substitution of an English /r/. Postvocalic trilled /r/ occurs in German in some dialects, in stage pronunciation, and, in general, after short vowels. But coming from a foreigner it will be interpreted as evidence of a foreign accent. With a pronunciation problem caused by a combination of phonetic and orthographic interferences, it may be advisable to use a special type of symbol (rather than traditional orthography) to represent the sound, at least in the initial stages of the course. This is done automatically if the teacher relies on a phonemic transcription or a phonetic alphabet (rather than on orthography) in the beginning of the course. Yet most experienced teachers of German find that the German normal sound-symbol relationship is regular enough to make phonetic or phonemic transcriptions unnecessary. But even if normal orthography is used, a sort of special symbol can be introduced to remind the pupil **not** to use the English reflex for /r/ in German. The teacher may use consistently a special or somewhat unusual way of writing *r* (e.g., Ω or R).

Before leaving the discussion of general categories of pronunciation problems, we should finally point out that at times mispronunciation may be simply the result of a fear of sounding "different" (non-American) and that often the student who is capable of correct pronunciation may mispronounce because of sloppiness and lack of attention. In either case, encouragement on the part of the teacher will help.

Let us now take a brief look at the German and English sound systems and first isolate the genuine pronunciation problems the teacher may expect.

(B) CONSONANTS

The following list gives all the consonant (and semivowel) phonemes of standard German, with examples for occurrence in different positions:

/p/	*Pein*	*Raupe*	*blieb*	*Haupt*
/b/	*Bein*	*Haube*		
/t/	*Teig*	*hatte*	*Tat*	*Rad*
/d/	*dein*	*baden*		
/k/	*kein*	*Hacke, Haken*	*lag*	*Sack*
/g/	*gern*	*Wage*		
/f/	*fern, fein*	*rufen*	*rief*	
/v/	*Wasser*	*Löwe*		
/s/	*Stil*	*Wasser, reissen,*	*nass*	*gross*
/z/	*sitzen*	*Rose*		
/ʃ/	*schon*	*rauschen*	*Rausch*	
/ʒ/	(*Genie*	*Garage*)		
/ç/	*Chemie*	*sicher*	*dich*	
/x/		*wachen*	*Dach*	
/m/	*mein*	*wimmern*	*wem*	
/n/	*nein*	*Sonne*	*ihn*	
/ŋ/		*singen*	*sang*	
/l/	*Leib*	*wollen*	*weil*	
/r/	*Rache*	*wehren*	*Wert, wir Geschirr*	
/j/	*ja*	*Koje*		
/h/	*Hose*	*wohin*		

Although we are primarily concerned with the presentation of the German phonemes, not with the phonemic analysis of the language (problems of phonemic analysis are comparatively few), we might question the existence of the phoneme /ʒ/ for German, since almost all the examples of the phoneme (*Genie, Garage, Giro, Rage,* etc.) are borrowed from Romance languages, primarily French. Yet since all of those words can be used as part of the standard German vocabulary and must be learned by the student, it would serve little purpose to eliminate the /ʒ/ phoneme.

Another linguistic consideration concerns the status of /x/ (*ach*) and /ç/ (*ich*) as separate phonemes. For all practical purposes, the two sounds are in complementary distribution: /x/ occurs after the central and back vowels (*a, o, u, au*, etc.), whereas /ç/ is reserved for the other positions. The possibility of a contrastive distribution of /ç/ and /x/ rests on the fact that speakers of standard German will use the /ç/ (*ich*-sound) in the diminutive ending regardless of the phonetic environment. Thus, *Kuhchen* (*little cow*) or *Tauchen* (*little rope*) as diminutives of *Kuh* and *Tau* are pronounced with the *ich*-sound, whereas *Kuchen* (*cake*) and *tauchen* (*dive*) are produced with the expected *ach*-sound. This is small evidence on which to set up separate phonemes (the writer of the book, although a native speaker of German, has never used the words *Kuhchen* and *Tauchen*). But from the pedagogical point of view, it is preferable and perhaps

	Bilabial	Labio-Dental	Dental	Alveolar	Alveo-Palatal	Velar	Uvular
GERMAN stop	p, b		t, d			k, g	
fricative: slit groove		f, v	s, z		ç ʃ ʒ	(glottal: h)	
lateral			l				
vibrant							R
nasal	m		n			ɲ	
semivowels					j		
ENGLISH stop	p, b			t, d		k, g	
affricate					č, ǰ		
fricative: slit groove		f, v	θ, ð	s, z	ʃ ʒ	(glottal: h)	
lateral				l			
nasal	m			n		ŋ	
semivowels	w			r	j		

necessary to distinguish the sounds, and therefore a phonemic transcription using different symbols for the sounds has pedagogical advantages, even if the separation into two phonemes may be linguistically somewhat doubtful.

In order to compare the German and English consonant and semivowel phonemes, we may use the chart on the preceding page.

Comparison of the Systems

1. The comparison of the sound systems shows that there are really only three German consonants that we could classify as completely foreign to the American student, namely the sounds /x/, /ç/, and /r/. In the case of the last-mentioned, the fact that English also has an /r/ phoneme should not deceive us about the completely different nature of the German sound.

As far as the /x/ phoneme is concerned, American students are likely to substitute the closest sound of their own system—namely /k/. Practically all of the students making the mistake will **hear** that their substitute sound is incorrect, in other words, that they are saying *nackt* instead of *Nacht*, or *Dock* instead of *doch*. It may be helpful to contrast pairs, such as *taugt* ≠ *taucht* or *dick* ≠ *dich*, to make the student quite aware of the difference. Then he must go through the exercise of releasing the obstacle of the /k/ sound in words like *Sack*, *nackt*, *lockt* so that he learns to produce a continuant sound at the point of articulation of the velar stop.

The sounds that students are most likely to substitute in their mispronunciation of the /ç/ sound are its closest neighbors, a palatal variety of /k/: for example, *dick* instead of *dich*, or the grooved fricative /ʃ/ which corresponds to the ungrooved slit fricative /ç/, *misch* instead of *mich*. It is important to make the student aware of the difference between /ç/ and /k/, as in *dich* ≠ *dick* /diç ≠ dik/, and /ç/ and /ʃ/, as in *mich* ≠ *misch* /miç ≠ miʃ/.

Either one of the "substitute" sounds is a good place from which to start the teaching of the /ç/ sound. The student can be trained to give up the occlusion of the /k/ of *dick* (by "blowing the air" through the obstacle formed in the production of /k/); or he can be asked to produce the /ʃ/ (*misch*) and then be shown how by slightly flattening his tongue he can reach the pronunciation of /ç/ (*mich*). The latter procedure, which implies drill in the contrast /ʃ/ ≠ /ç/, has the advantage that it also points out and takes care of the pronunciation problem created by the fact that many Americans pronounce /ʃ/ (*misch*) with much less grooving of the tongue than is required by German. Since in English the grooved fricative /ʃ/ is not contrasted with the ungrooved slit fricative /ç/—pronounced at the same point of articulation—the speaker of English can be sloppy about the amount of grooving in the pronunciation of /ʃ/. If this sloppiness is brought into German, the phonemic contrast /ʃ/ ≠ /ç/ (*misch* ≠ *mich*) may become blurred.

A look at our chart will tell us that there is one more likely candidate that can serve as a base from which to approach the pronunciation of the /ç/ phoneme: the semivowel /j/ (as in *yes, ja, jeder*). It has the same point of articulation as /ç/. Involved in the conversion of /j/ to /ç/ is a process of unvoicing and producing greater "friction noise." Therefore the teaching of /ç/ can be approached from the sound many Americans produce at the beginning of words such as *huge, humor, Hugh* (where the combination /h/ + /j/ [*hju*] makes for an unvoiced hissing pronunciation of /j/); or the student can be asked to pronounce words like *yes, ja, je* while strongly blowing air through the narrowing in the speech organs created during the pronunciation of the /j/.

As far as the pronunciation of German /r/ is concerned, the teacher must first decide whether to teach the uvular [R] or the apical flap, or trill, still advocated by some authorities as the presumed standard or "original" German /r/. Our own recommendation is to teach the uvular and give the student the option of using the apical sound if the uvular [R] turns out to be too difficult. This recommendation is based on two considerations: **most** educated Germans use a uvular [R]; and although the apical [r] is used by **many** Germans, from the mouth of a foreigner it will be interpreted as additional evidence of a foreign accent and **not** as a variety of a German pronunciation. At the same time, however, the apical [r] is undoubtedly more acceptable than the English retroflex semivowel, and for some American students it seems easier to learn the apical rather than the uvular [R], probably because American English speech has at least one sound that is quite close to the apical flap: the pronunciation of *tt* and *dd*, as in *better* and *ladder*. Therefore the student can be told to pronounce the *tt* of *Bitte* or *Zettel* in "American fashion" and can be led from there to the pronunciation of *wirre, zerren* (or perhaps English words, such as *better, kitty, witty*, can be taken as the starting point). Another possibility of approaching the apical [r] is to let the student pronounce sequences like *gdo, gde*, then lead him to the pronunciation of *gross, Griess*, and so on.

Yet initially we should always insist on teaching the pronunciation of the uvular [R]. The problem is that English has no similar sound from which to approach the teaching of the uvular [R]. If the student already knows how to pronounce the German /x/ (*ach*), then this can serve as the starting point. By contrasting words like *dach* ≠ *dar*, or having the student say pairs like (*xau*) ≠ *frau*, (*xo*) ≠ *froh*, the teacher can try to get the student to voice the /x/ and push the point of articulation slightly back to reach the [R] pronunciation; or he can simply advise the student to imitate a "gargling noise," and thus produce the uvular friction involved in the production of /R/.

Another problem of the production of /r/, which has to be faced regardless of whether an apical /r/ or a uvular [R] has been taught, is the pronunciation of the postvocalic variant. Here German uses an unrounded central/back vowel: [ʌ]. Thus *der*, *wehrt*, are in fact pronounced [deʌ], ve:ʌ t]. The sound [ʌ] itself is not difficult for the American student. It is like the sound produced by many speakers of English in the word *but*, or in the second syllable of *sofa*. Actually there are only two problems the American student faces in connection with postvocalic [ʌ]. First of all, he may have trouble distinguishing (in hearing and pronunciation) the German final (unstressed) –er from –e—that is, he may confuse *bitte* and *bitter* [bi̧tə, bi̧tʌ]. Thus special discrimination and pronunciation exercises may be needed to teach this distinction, to which we shall return briefly in our discussion of the vowels. Second, the student may simply transpose his pronunciation of the initial *r* to the postvocalic position. This quite comprehensible tendency must be counteracted by contrastive drills in which words like *führen* ≠ *für* [fü:Rən ≠ fü:ʌ] or *mehren* ≠ *mehr* [mȩ:Rən ≠ mȩ:ʌ] are contrasted for the students. In connection with such drills, it should also be pointed out that for most Germans the rule that [ʌ] and not [R] be used in postvocalic positions does in fact not apply after short vowels: thus *zieren* ≠ *zier* [tsi̧:Rən ≠ tsi̧:ʌ], but *irren/irr* [i̧Rən/i̧R].

2. In the category of "near substitute" sounds that the American student might use in German, we must, above all, consider the sound /l/. German /l/ is an alveolar sound, produced with the tip of the tongue against the alveolar ridge. Some Americans produce such an /l/, at least in some positions; but many Americans have the habit of "velarizing" the /l/ sound. Instead of making contact with the tip of the tongue against the alveolar ridge, they draw the tongue back against the velum. The result is the so-called "dark" /l/ sound, which to the German is a sure sign of the English accent. The student must therefore be made to hear the difference between the German /l/ and his own substitute, primarily by making him listen to contrastive German-English pairs like *hell* ≠ *hell*, *Ball* ≠ *ball*, *viel* ≠ *feel*, and so on. Then the articulation of the German /l/ must be clearly explained and practiced.

3. Our third category of pronunciation mistakes concerns sounds that the student can easily pronounce but that may nevertheless be difficult in certain positions, in which they may be mispronounced. In this category are the unvoiced stops, /p/, /t/, /k/. In initial position the German and English pronunciations are identical. In intervocalic position or in word-final position, there may be differences. The German intervocalic /p/, /t/, /k/ or the final /p/, /t/, /k/ are pronounced very much like the initial ones: fully articulated stops followed by a slight puff of air (aspiration). In the English intervocalic pronunciation (or in the position before an unstressed vowel after a consonant), the aspiration may be missing, for example, *p, t, k* in *happy, hamper, city, beauty, bounty, lanky, talking*. In the final position, English stops are often unreleased: the speech organs are closed and the air comes up against the closure; but instead of the air pressure against the closure producing a plosive noise, the closure is released slowly and the sound, so to speak, fizzles out (such as /p/, /t/, /k/ in *cap, hit, luck*. In the case of the phoneme /t/ in intervocalic position, an additional problem may arise as the result of the habit of some students to produce a flap sound. This flap—quick hitting of the alveoli with the tip of the tongue—is usually produced before an unstressed vowel and is also accompanied by the blurring or loss of distinction between /-t-/ and /-d-/ (*latter* pronounced like *ladder*). The introduction of this speech habit into German (*bitter* pronounced with the flap of American *ladder*) is an unacceptable pronunciation. Therefore the student must be trained to produce all German /p/, /t/, /k/ phonemes—intervocalic and final—with great care and transfer his pronunciation of initial /p/, /t/, /k/ (*Panne, Tag, Kanne*) to all other positions. This is usually not a major problem, provided the student is made to hear the difference between what he should be saying and his various mispronunciations. Thus English–German contrasts like *cup* ≠ *ab, hat* ≠ *hat, lock* ≠ *lag*, can be used to make the student aware of the fully released final consonants. The difference between English flapped or inaspirated intervocalic stops and the corresponding fully pronounced aspirated German sounds can be shown by opposing words like *better* ≠ *Betten, wacky* ≠ *wacker, happy* ≠ *Mappe*.

Another instance in which the American student mispronounces a German consonant, although he is able to produce it perfectly well in most positions, is the voiced pronunciation of final *g, b, d*. German normally unvoices all final consonants, so that words like *Sieg, Raub, Bad, Rad*, although spelled with final *g, b, d*, are in fact pronounced with final /k/, /p/, /t/.

The student's mispronunciation is due primarily to the orthography of German, which does not take into consideration the change in voicing /g / k/, /b / p/, /d / t/—involved in alternations such as *Siege ≠ Sieg*, *Räuber ≠ Raub*, *Räder ≠ Rad*. Some students also experience difficulty in pronouncing certain German consonant clusters. Here it is probably only the cluster *kn* (such as *Knie* mispronounced [kəni], with a vowel between *k* and *n*) that may represent a real pronunciation problem to some students.

The failure to pronounce *k* in the combination *kn* (*Knie, Knochen*) is also the result of the influence of English orthography, in which the *k* of the *kn* combination has become silent. Other mispronunciations of clusters (*Spiel* as [spi:l] instead of [ʃpi:l]; *zu* as [zu̥] instead of [tsu̥:]) are probably due to the influence of orthography rather than to problems caused by English articulatory habits.

4. Mispronunciation of German consonant phonemes due to the influence of orthography includes, first of all, a group of errors caused by the importation of English sound-symbol relationships into German: the letter *w* pronounced as /w/ instead of /v/—for example, *Wasser* mispronounced as [wạs ʌ] instead of [vạs ʌ]. The letters *qu* pronounced as /kw/ instead of /kv/—*Qual* mispronounced as [kwạ:l] instead of [kvạ:l]. Although the combination /kv/ is nonexistent in English, its pronunciation does not seem to be difficult for the student. The error, if it occurs, seems due almost entirely to the orthographic influence. The letter *v* may be pronounced as [v] instead of [f]—*Vieh* pronounced [vi̥:] instead of [fi̥:]. As mentioned above, *z* may be mispronounced as [z] instead of [ts]—*zu* pronounced as [zu̥:] instead of [tsu̥:]. Another possible mispronunciation —though quite rare—which might occur under the influence of English orthography is that of *ch* as [č] rather than [ç] or [x]. In the category of rather rare mispronunciation is also the reflex [ǰ] for the letter *j* (instead of [j]).

All of these mispronunciations are, of course, due to the pupil's pronouncing what he sees. As stated earlier, the remedy lies in establishing and drilling correct pronunciation **before** the pupil meets the orthographic representation of the word. If the mistakes occur in spite of previous audio-lingual training after orthography has been introduced, then specific reading and spelling exercises must be used: for example, the student mispronouncing *w* as [w] must be made to read and write series of words, such as *wer, wissen, Wasser, Wein*.

Some "spelling pronunciations," or rather mispronunciations, are due to inconsistencies within German orthography or to a combination of German inconsistency with the influence of English orthography.

Thus the mispronunciation of words like *Spiel, Stand,* as [spi̧ːl] [sta̧nt] rather than [ʃpi̧ːl] [ʃta̧nt] is due to the influence of the English pronunciation of *st, sp,* as well as the failure of German to indicate the /ʃ/ pronunciation by the symbol normally associated with it (namely, *sch*). In the same category belongs the already mentioned failure of German orthography to indicate the voiceless nature of consonants in word (syllable) final position if they happen to be voiced in other environments: *Liebe* [li̧ːbə] but *lieb* [li̧ːp], *Tage* [ta̧ːgə] but *Tag* [ta̧ːk]. Here, too, the student may use the normal American reflex (the voiced consonant) because of the German orthography; but an initial audio-lingual attack may eliminate or at least minimize the problem. If mispronunciation under the influence of orthography does occur, extensive reading and writing drill is indicated; for example, the student should read and write series of words such as *spielen, spinnen, sperren, Spange,* etc., or practice the voiced/unvoiced alternations in pairs like *Räder ≠ Rad, Tage ≠ Tag, Preise ≠ Preis,* or *leben ≠ lebte, legen ≠ legte, weben ≠ webte, sagen ≠ sagte,* or *bleiben ≠ blieb, schreiben ≠ schrieb,* and so forth.

Another example of an inconsistency within an inconsistency in German orthography sound relation concerns the ending *–ig.* Standard German pronunciation requires here the reflex /iç/, for instance, *König* /köːniç/. In other words, the *g* orthography normally corresponding to the sound /g/ should, according to the rule of final unvoicing, stand for /k/, but it does, in standard German at least, stand for /ç/ in the *–ig* combination. However, the pronunciation /ik/ for *–ig* is used in large parts of Germany (the entire south and Austria), so that the same pronunciation by the American student seems reasonably acceptable.

Other inconsistencies in the German orthographic representation of consonants are quite minor and offer few if any problems in pronunciation: /ts/ is normally represented by *z* as in *zu,* sometimes by *tz* (*platzen*) and in somewhat antiquated orthography by *c* (in words of non-German origin, for instance, *Cicero*). As a final inconsistency we can note that German orthography indicates the so-called short vowels of German by the orthographic doubling of the following consonant. It would be a mistake to interpret this orthographic double consonant as a genuine double or long consonant in speech. It is only a device to indicate something about the nature of the preceding vowel. Within this orthographic convention of doubling the consonant to indicate the short vowel are again minor inconsistencies: instead of a double *kk,* German orthography uses *ck* (*Haken, Hacke*; note that the latter word would be divided as *Hak-ke*).

Because German *ss* between vowels indicates shortness of the preceding vowel and single *s* between vowels indicates a voiced *s*-sound (/z/ as in *Hase, Rose*), some types of German orthography use a special symbol (ß—"*scharfes* s") to indicate the unvoiced *s*-sound after long vowels in intervocalic position. Thus, *Hase* /hązə/, *Masse* /mąsə/, but Maße /mąsə/; ß is also used to indicate unvoiced /s/ in all other positions: *Schluß, muß, mußte, Grieß*, and so forth.

(C) VOWELS

The following list gives the German vowel phonemes with corresponding examples:

/i̯/	*Wiese*	*Wien, ihn*
/i̯/	*wissen*	*gewinne, in*
/ę/	*Wesen*	*wen*
/ę/	*wessen*	*Welle, wenn*
/u̯/	*Busse*	*Fuss*
/u̯/	*Russe*	*Schluss*
	(Russian)	
/o̧/	*Rose*	*bloss*
/o̧/	*Schlosser*	*Ross*
/ą/	*Rasen, Hase*	*sass*
/ą/	*Rasse*	*nass*
/ɛ:/	*gäbe*	
/ɛ/	*hätte*	
/ü/	*Lüge*	*Gefühl*
/ü/	*Mücke*	*Stück*
/ö̧/	*Höhle*	*Föhn*
/ö̧/	*Hölle*	*könnt*

The following phoneme exists only in unstressed position:

/ə/	*gesprochen*	*arbeitete*

German has, in addition, the following diphthongs:

/ai/	*mein*	*Leib, Laib*
/o̧i/	*Leute*	*Häute*
/au/	*Laut*	*Haut*

Thus if we except the phonemes /ɛ:/ and /ɛ/—the so-called "umlaut *ä*," which many Germans in fact do not distinguish from /ę/ and /ę/ (*bete* and *bäte* pronounced alike)—and the phoneme /ə/, which exists only in the unaccented position, we find that the German vowel phonemes occur in the following corresponding pairs:

$$a, a \quad e, e \quad i, i \quad o, o \quad u, u \quad ö, ö \quad ü, ü$$

The vowels in each pair are distinguished from each other in several ways:

1.   With the exception of the pair /a/, /a/ (where this relationship is reversed), the first vowel of each pair is pronounced with a tongue position slightly higher than the one used for the second one.

2.   The second vowel in each pair is produced with a tongue position slightly more to the center of the mouth cavity.

3.   The first vowel in each pair is produced with greater tension in the speech organs.

4.   In stressed position—but in stressed position only—the first vowel is longer than the second.

For the reason mentioned in paragraph 4, we conventionally distinguish the vowels in each pair as long versus short. We should note, however, that this distinction is applicable only in the **stressed** position. The vowels of the first syllable of *Konzert* and *Columbus* are not pronounced the same but are both short (the *o* of *Columbus* is tense, the *o* of *Konzert* is lax). Most linguists prefer to present the main difference, or phonemic difference, between the members of the pairs above in terms of the phonetic distinction that is consistently maintained, namely, **tense versus lax**. The distinction between the lax (short) and tense (long) vowels is obviously a phonemic one: *Masse* ≠ *Maße*, *bieten* ≠ *bitten*. The rule (found in many textbooks) that short vowels occur before double consonants states a convention of German orthography (useful in spelling and in the reading attack on unknown words), but is not consistent enough to be relied upon. What we can state from the linguistic point of view, however, is that the contrast between tense and lax vowels or the distribution of certain vowels is subject to certain restrictions. Thus the lax vowels do not, normally at least, occur in syllable-final position (possible exceptions are interjections such as *na, ja, naja*). At the end of the syllable only the long vowel is possible: *Sie, je-der, wo*, and so on. Furthermore, we can remember that /ə/ occurs only as an unstressed vowel and that a contrast between lax /a/ and tense /a/ is not maintained in unaccent position.

In order to discuss the difficulties offered by the German vowel system, let us turn to a very brief and somewhat simplified consideration of the vowels of American English. Here we can again first list the phonemes. In considering the list, the reader should keep in mind that many highly diphthongal sounds like the vowels in *beat, bone, bait,* and *food* are interpreted as single phonemes (see p. 60).

/i/	*beat*	/ə/	*but, better, enough*	Diphthongs:	
/ɪ/	*bit*	/ɔ/	*bought*	/ai/	*bite*
/e/	*bait*	/o/	*bone*	/oi/	*coin*
/ę/	*bet*	/ʉ/	*good*	/au/	*clown*
/æ/	*bat*	/u/	*food*		
/a/	*hot, pot*				

Obviously these phonemes are produced differently in different regions of the United States. The words *hot* and *pot* are not produced with an /a/ phoneme in some regions of the country (*father* may be a better example for an /a/ phoneme in parts of New England). The phoneme /ə/ includes a wide range of sounds: It is not only the sound that appears in stressed position in *but, rough, enough,* or *bluff,* but also the unstressed sound of *enough* or *sofa.* Since the stressed and unstressed pronunciations can—obviously—not be used to contrast with each other, we may interpret them as variations of the same phoneme.

American English has furthermore a tendency to lose certain vowel distinctions in specific positions. Since this tendency will play a role in our evaluation of the student's difficulty in German, these losses of distinction should be mentioned very briefly. First of all, some Americans have—depending on the dialect—a tendency to obliterate vowel distinctions before the consonant *r.* Some will distinguish the /i/ of *nearer* from the /ɪ/ of *mirror*; others will pronounce the same /i/ in both words. In many parts of the United States, a distinction is made between *Mary* /meri/, *merry* /męri/, and *marry* /mæri/. In some areas, *Mary* and *merry* are pronounced alike, and in large areas of the Middle West, you will hear the same /e/ sound in the first three words of the sentence *Merry Mary married John.* The second blurring of vowel distinction concerns the use of the /ə/ sound in unaccented position instead of other vowels. The details of this blurring need not concern us here. But it is possible, for example, to pronounce *delicious* as /di'liʃəs/, yet in rapid speech we are more likely to say /də'liʃəs/. The vowel pronounced [æ] in *grammar* /græmər/ becomes /ə/ in *grammatical* /grəmætikəl/ if the syllable in which it occurs is not under stress. Similar switches from other vowels to /ə/ can be observed if we contrast the word *compare* /kəmper/ with *incomparable* /inkampərəbl/ or the stressed pronunciation of *do* [du] with its

possible unstressed pronunciation in a sentence like *What do you do?*
/wat də ju du/.

Putting the two vowel systems—German and English—next to each
other, we obtain the following picture: (Vowels are arranged according
to tongue position during production, see p. 57).

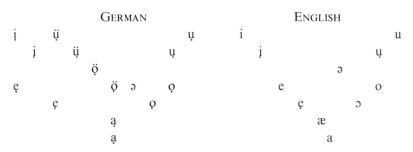

Using the various types of categories of conflicts between systems we
have isolated before, we can first turn our attention to those vowels which
have no real counterparts in English.

1. The vowels of German /ü̲/ /ü/; /ö̲/, /ö/ belong in this first category
of completely new sounds. If the student substitutes at all, he might use
/i̲/ for /ü/ (*Tier* instead of *Tür*), an obvious error. For the German /ö̲/ the
student may try to substitute the /ə/ phoneme of English—which especially
before *r* has a pronunciation somewhat reminiscent of /ö̲/ (German *Töne*
pronounced with the vowel of English *turn*). It is not a very good substitution. The English sound is more central and not produced with the distinct
lip-rounding characteristic of the German /ö̲/ sound. Therefore the student
who is not able to achieve the correct pronunciation of /ü/ and /ö̲/ by
imitation must receive special drill. It may be necessary to make him hear
the difference between German /ö̲/ and the English /ə + r/ sound, for
instance, contrast *turn* with *Töne*, *bursar* with *böse*, *fern* with *Föhn*,
learn with *Löhne*. More important, the student must be made to realize
that German /ü̲/, /ü/; /ö̲/, /ö/ are in fact /i̲/, /i/; /e̲/, /e/ produced with lip-
rounding, or /u̲/, /u/; /o̲/, /o/ produced with the tongue in front rather
than in the back of the oral cavity. The change from /u̲/, /u/; /o̲/, /o/
to /ü̲/, /ü/; /ö̲/, /ö/ can be practiced by having the pupil go through
the singular/plural alternation of many German nouns, for example
Zug ≠ Züge; *Mutter ≠ Mütter*, *Ton ≠ Töne*, *Rock ≠ Röcke*. It must
be pointed out to the pupil that in the vowel of the second member of each
such pair, he must keep the same lip-rounding as before, and that the
change in the stressed vowel is simply due to a forward shift of the tongue.
The reverse approach to the umlaut vowels starts with nouns like *Ziege*,

Kissen, Sehne, kenne, which can be turned into *Züge, Küssen, Söhne,* or *könne* by simply superimposing lip-rounding on the stressed vowel.

2. The other problems in the German vowel system belong essentially in the category where a close but more or less unacceptable substitute derived from the American vowel system may be used.

Here we should mention first the problem of the tense (long) German /i̜/, /e̜/, /o̜/, /u̜/ sounds. The sounds the American students are most likely to substitute are the English phonemes /i/, /e/, /o/, /u/ as in *see, gay, boat, do.* If we compare the vowel sounds of these words with those of German words using the corresponding German vowels, the problem or error involved in the substitution becomes quite clear: *see ≠ sie, gay ≠ geh, boat ≠ Boot, do ≠ du.* The English vowels are produced with definite upglides—in other words, they are highly diphthongal. The German sounds have no such diphthongal quality and the substitution of the English diphthongal type of sound is to the German ear one of the most characteristic features of the American-English accent. Corrective drill consists primarily of making the student aware of the difference by contrasting German and English words containing the vowels between which he must learn to differentiate: *knee ≠ nie; fee ≠ Vieh; do ≠ du, shoe ≠ Schuh; bait ≠ Beet, gay ≠ geh, say ≠ See.* The student must also learn not to change the pronunciation (tongue height or lip-rounding) during the pronunciation of the vowel. In the pronunciation of English /u/, /o/, /i/, /e/, lip-rounding or spreading takes place **during** the pronunciation of the vowel and is associated with the diphthongal quality of the sound. Thus one way the student can be kept from imitating these speech habits in German is to have him anticipate the rounding or spreading of lips during the pronunciation of the consonants which precede the vowel. If the lips are rounded before the /d/ of *du* is pronounced, or spread before the /s/ of *sie* is produced, it is unlikely that the student will produce the diphthongal English vowels.

Next in order of difficulty and persistence as American accent come the student's possible problems with the German /a̜/, /a̱/, and /o̜/ sounds. A look at the chart of vowels will make clear that the student is, in fact, not prepared to deal with a phonemic contrast between the sounds /a̱/ and /a̜/. With German /i̜/, /e̜/, /o̜/, /u̜/ versus /i̱/, /e̱/, /o̱/, /u̱/, the student has normally no perception problems because English, like German, distinguishes two sets which, although pronounced quite differently, can at least be equated when it comes to perception. However, American English has only one /a/ phoneme. Nevertheless, students can usually be made aware of the allophonic length difference in the /a/ phoneme caused by the voiced or voiceless character of the following consonant: *hot* ≠ *hod*, *cop* ≠ *cob*, *pot* ≠ *pod*. Still, the German contrast /ạ/ ≠ /ą/ (as in *Stadt* ≠ *Staat*) may be missed by the student, and auditory discrimination exercises pointing to contrasts like *Stadt* ≠ *Staat*, *Hacken* ≠ *Haken*, or *satt* ≠ *Saat* may be necessary. The exact nature of the sound that the American student may substitute for the German /ạ/, /ą/ will vary considerably according to his American dialect. The substitution of the /a/ in *father* for German /ą/ will usually furnish a sound that is too long and drawn. The substitution of a short variety of English /a/, as in *cot*, for /ą/ will furnish a sound that is lower than the German /ą/ and does not have its lax quality. The phoneme /ə/, as in *but*, is, as we mentioned earlier, produced over a considerable **allophonic** range. Thus some variations of it may come very close to the German /ạ/ and furnish another possible (but not very acceptable) substitute. Depending on the nature of the student's problem, the teacher may wish to make him aware of the contrast between German /ạ/ and /ą/ and the various American vowel substitutes; for instance, to avoid the substitution of English /a/ for German /ą/, we can drill the contrast /a/ ≠ /ą/ in words like *far* ≠ *fahr*, *tot* ≠ *Tat*. To combat the substitution of English /ə/ for German /ạ/ we can contrast words like *come* ≠ *komm*, *but* ≠ *hat*, and point out to the student that the vowel of *hat* is slightly lower and more forward than English /ə/ in *but*.

Most Americans may have difficulty as far as the German /ǫ/ is concerned. The /ɔ/ sound of *caught*, *ball*, *saw* will normally be quite a bit longer and lower than the German lax /ǫ/ of *Schloss* or *voll*. The student must be made aware of the difference between the German /ǫ/ and his substitute sound by contrasting English and German words, such as *fall* ≠ *voll*, *tall* ≠ *toll*, *cost* ≠ *Kost*, and so on.

3. As we have discussed earlier, a special set of problems is created by the tendency of American English to lose certain vowel contrasts in specific positions, namely, after *r* and in unstressed position. Losing the contrast means that a distinction between certain sounds, although made easily in other positions, is neither heard nor made (technical term: **neutralized**) in the above positions. The speaker of American English has, as it were, a "blind spot" for certain contrasts before *r* or in the unaccented syllable. This blind spot might be brought into German. The student who can easily distinguish between the /ị/ and /i̧/ of *bitte* and *biete* may have trouble hearing and producing the difference between *irr* and *ihr*, and the student who would certainly distinguish /a/ and /e/ in stressed position may pronounce the German word *Kaffee* /kạfẹ/ with the stress on the

first syllable, as [kafə], and the word *Komma* /kǫma/ with the blurred /ə/ sound in the final syllable, as [kǫmə].

In order to combat the problem of blurring vowel differences before *r*, the student may need contrasting drills for all of the German tense ≠ lax pairs, as well as the rounded front vowels /ü/, /ü̧/; /ö/, /ö̧/, with their rounded back or unrounded front counterparts, for instance:

ihr ≠ irr, wir ≠ wirr	i̧ ≠ i̧		
führen ≠ murren, Kur ≠ kurz	ü ≠ ü̧	u̧ ≠ u̧	
vor ≠ fort	ǫ ≠ ǫ		
fahre ≠ Pfarre, Haare ≠ harre	a̧ ≠ a̧		
Heer ≠ Herr, sehr ≠ zerr, spüre ≠ Sperre	ȩ ≠ ȩ	ü ≠ ȩ	
Tür ≠ Tier, Tour	ü ≠ i̧	u̧	
würde ≠ wird, wurde	ü ≠ i̧	u̧	
Wörter ≠ Worte, Werte	ö ≠ ǫ	ȩ	
Föhre ≠ Pforte, Fähre	ö̧ ≠ ǫ	ȩ (ε:)	

In addition, it may also be necessary to contrast the German sounds with the possible English substitutes—English /i/ ≠ German /i̧/: *dear ≠ Tier, fear ≠ vier*; English /u/ ≠ German /u̧/: *poor ≠ nur, tour ≠ Uhr*; English /e/ ≠ German /ȩ/: *dare ≠ der, lair ≠ leer*; English /o/ ≠ German /ǫ/: *ore ≠ Ohr, more ≠ Moor*.

In connection with all of these discrimination exercises, it must be stressed that they cannot be dissociated from the student's acquisition of the correct German *r*-sound. As long as the student substitutes the English /r/ for the German sound, the teaching of the vowels preceding it will be largely futile, and the acquisition of a correct German /r/ will in turn take care of many of the student's problems with the preceding vowel sound.

The American-English tendency to blur vowel distinctions in unaccented syllables makes itself felt in various areas of German pronunciation. First of all, Americans may have difficulty hearing and pronouncing the difference between the /ə/ sound and the German [ʌ] allophone of /r/. *Bitte ≠ bitter, Werte ≠ werter, leite ≠ Leiter*, may all become alike. This difficulty arises because the American /ə/ sound ranges phonetically over a wide field, encompassing both the German /ə/ of *bitte* /bi̧tə/ and the [ʌ] variants of /r/, such as [bi̧t ʌ]. In this case, contrasting drill between pairs like *bitte ≠ bitter* or *Werte ≠ werter* may be necessary to create a phonemic boundary where there is none in English. In a similar way, the wide phonetic spread of the /ə/ sound in English may make the student lose the phonemic contrast between German /ə/ and the unstressed /i̧/

sound: *Königen* (ending /-ən/) and *Königin* (ending /-ịn/) may become alike in perception and speech. Here, too, phonemic awareness may have to be created by contrasting drill: *Köchin ≠ Köchen, Königin ≠ Königen.*

The tendency to blur vowels other than /i/, /ə/, or [ʌ] into one /ə/ sound will affect the student's pronunciation primarily in the case of words of non-German origin, to so-called "*Fremdwörter.*" These words are, however, quite frequent. In addition, they are quite often Latin or Greek words which have also been adopted into English—one more reason that the student is likely to carry over the English pronunciation habit of using /ə/ instead of another vowel. This tendency is best counteracted by overtly contrasting the English and German pronunciation:

ENGLISH	GERMAN
sofa	*Sofa*
Anna	*Anna*
maximum	*Maximum*
automatic	*automatisch*
collapse	*Kollaps*

Another problem that frequently arises with the German "*Fremd-wörter*" is that the corresponding English word is stressed on a different syllable: English *democracy* [di′makrəsi],[1] with stress on the *o*; German *Demokratie* [dẹmọkra′tị], with stress on the final syllable. This problem, however, leads us into the discussion of stress and intonation and is, in fact, not connected with a difficulty offered by the individual sounds as such.

4. Pronunciation problems caused by the influence of orthography are comparatively few. German orthography is fairly consistent in using *a, e, i, o, u, ü, ö* for the lax (short) vowels if they are followed orthographically by more than one consonant symbol. The tense (long) counterparts of the vowels are indicated either by there being only one consonant symbol after the vowel, or by special devices to indicate length: the *e* of *ie* or the *h* symbol. In a few cases, doubling of the vowel is used to indicate length, as in *Beet* or *Boot*. The symbols used for the vowels or diphthongs themselves are also fairly unambiguous and consistent, with very rare exceptions—two symbols, *ei* and *ai*, are used for the /ai/ diphthong: *Leib* (*body*), but *Laib* (*loaf*). In a similar way there are two symbols for the /oi/ diphthong: *heute*, but *Häuser*. And since, as mentioned earlier, many Germans do not pronounce *ä* (the "umlaut ä") differently from the *e*-sound (*Bäche* with the same vowel as *Becher*; *währen* pronounced like

---

[1] Note that stress is marked by the stress symbol (′) being placed before the stressed syllable.

wehren), we may consider *ä* and *e* as alternate spellings of the same sound. At the same time it is clear that the last two inconsistencies of German orthography are a blessing rather than a difficulty, because they make it clear to the pupil that words like *Bäche* or *Häuser* contain the same root as *Bach* or *Haus*, a fact which would be obscured by a phonetically consistent orthography (*Haus*, plural **Heuser*). As far as mispronunciation under the influence of English orthography is concerned, a beginning student may occasionally pronounce *ei* as /i/ (as in *receive*) or *i* as /ai/ (as in *mine*). Such mispronunciations are partly due to premature exposure to reading and can, when they occur, be corrected by writing exercises contrasting series such as *mein, dein, sein* with *Bibel, Fibel, Liter*.

(D) INTONATION

Of all the languages taught in the school curriculum, German is probably the one which in the use of stress and intonation resembles English the most.

The differences between English and German intonation are of fairly subtle nature. The interplay between German intonation and word order is perhaps one of the most rewarding and interesting problems of linguistic research. However, German intonation as such is not one of the more serious teaching problems on the elementary levels. We can thus be fairly brief in describing the features that characterize both English and German intonation. The differences between the languages lie not in the features themselves, but only in the way in which they are employed. Both languages have the possibility of stressing or emphasizing any word within an utterance: $\overline{I}\lfloor know\ Charles.$ $I\lceil know\rfloor Charles.$ $I\ know\lceil Charles$; in a similar way: $Ich\lfloor kenne\ Karl.$ $Ich\lceil kenne\rfloor Karl.$ $Ich\ kenne\lceil Karl.$ Both languages have movable, phonemic, syntactical stress.

Aside from the syntactical stress, we can isolate in English as well as German at least three different degrees of loudness of stress within the word. If we compare the English words *discus* and *discuss* [ˈdiskəs, disˈkəs], we see that shifting the stress from the first to the second syllable changed the meaning. We have thus isolated one kind of word stress (**primary**) as opposed to another (**weak**). If we look at a pair like *animate* (adjective) and *animate* (verb) [ˈanimət, ˈaniˈmet], we can distinguish yet another degree of stress, a secondary stress, intermediate between the primary and the weak. The last syllable of the verb *animate* is stressed less loudly than the first—but stressed more strongly than the last syllable of the adjective. In German we can isolate similar differences in the loudness of stress.

There is obviously a difference between primary stress and weak stress, though pairs of the type *discus* and *discuss* are difficult to find (possible example: *Ideen* (*ideas*) and *Iden* (with stress on the first syllable, the *Ides* of March)). The intermediate level between the weak and primary stress can be shown by comparisons such as *Jahr Hundert* (primary stress on *Jahr*, as well as on the *u* of *Hundert*) and *Jahrhundert* (secondary stress on *Jahr*, primary stress on *hundert*).

Both English and German seem to operate with three contrastive degrees in the height of pitch. If we make the statement *I am going home*, we will usually begin on a medium level of pitch (No. 2). Then, on the word *home* the voice rises to a higher level (No. 3), and within the same word the pitch finally falls to a level below the one on which the sentence started (No. 1). The pitch contour of the sentence *I am going home* can thus be described as "2–3–1," or graphically presented as:

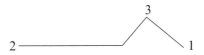

Similarly the intonation of the German sentence, *Ich gehe nach Hause*, can be described as a 2–3–1 pitch contour. Intonation patterns in both languages can therefore be described in terms of various sequences of three contrasting pitch levels: the question *Can you do this?* is likely to be pronounced with a pitch contour 2–3–3 (with the voice moving up in the last syllable). The question *Können Sie das machen?* is likely to follow a similar pattern. In a similar way, both languages follow intonation patterns resembling the patterns of statements if questions begin with a question word: *Where are you going? Wohin gehen Sie?*

Both German and English are finally characterized by having the possibility of different types of transition between sounds. The phonemic contrast between the two types in English is often illustrated by the difference in pronunciation of *nitrate* and *night rate*. In the word *nitrate*, all sounds are linked in closed **transition**, or **juncture**. In the phrase *night rate* there is a so-called **open juncture** between the *t* of *night* and the *r* of *rate*. German has the same possibility of marking boundaries in speech, for example, in the word *arbeitsam* we usually do not find any open juncture, but *Arbeitsamt* will normally be pronounced with open juncture between the *s* of *Arbeits* and the *a* of *amt*.

The problems the student encounters in German stress, pitch, or juncture are thus not caused by his having to learn any new phonemes. Whatever problems arise are due to the way in which the phonemes are used rather than to the phonemes themselves. Since the problems in pitch and juncture are fairly subtle, we shall not discuss them in a text concerned primarily with teaching problems encountered on the basic level. We shall, however, point out some of the problems connected with the use of stress.

The student's problem is not that he does not know how to stress but that he may simply misplace the stress or misjudge its significance. Perhaps the most important source of stress misplacement by the student lies in the German loan words that have English counterparts and in which English and German do not agree on the placement of primary stress:

ENGLISH	GERMAN
'atom	A'tom
ac'ademy	Akade'mie
bibli'ography	Bibliogra'phie

Even if the German and English words agree in the placement of the primary stress, the English word has often a secondary stress that is absent in German and that—if imported into German—distorts the German pronunciation: *philo'sophisch,* but `philo'sophical.*

In some instances the student's misplacement of primary stress may be due to his misapplication of a German pattern of shifting the stress, for example, in some words of foreign origin German shows a shift of stress in the noun inflection: *'Doktor,* plural *Dok'toren.* This may be misapplied by the student to words like *'Pfirsich, 'Pfirsiche*—or the reverse may happen: the student may pronounce *Doktoren* as *['dǫktǫrən], with a wrong primary stress on the first syllable. Many students may also find it difficult to use primary stress on the first syllable of long compounds. Generally the long German compound with initial primary stress does not correspond to the English stress pattern. Thus in words such as *Gunstbezeugung* /'gǔnstbə`tsǫigun̦/, *Anspruchslosigkeit* /'ǎnʃpruxs`lǫziçkaịt/, *Anhaltsplatz* /'ǎnhạlts`plạts/, the American student may shift the primary stress away from the first syllable or may at least try to introduce another primary stress on another syllable of the compound. Words of this type should be repeated several times when they are first introduced so that the correct sound (stress) pattern becomes firmly established.

Other stress problems have grammatical implications. In some instances German can assign a word to a different word class, depending on the stress that is employed. *Ein* with secondary stress is an indefinite article (*Ich habe ein|Buch|* = *I have a book*). *Ein* with primary—and syntactical—

stress is a numeral (*Ich habe| ein| Buch* = *I have one book*). *Der* with secondary stress is the article (*Der| Mann| ist hier*). The primary and syntactical stress converts the article to the demonstrative (*Der| Mann ist hier* = *that man is here*). Such uses of stress must be specifically contrasted and demonstrated to the student who might otherwise not use *der, die, das* as demonstratives—or fail to appreciate their significance if he hears them under syntactical stress.

Another grammatical type of stress problem deals with the German compound verb. Here it is extremely important that the student learn the correct stress, not only for the sake of the stress alone, but also for his correct usage of the verb in various tenses because he must remember that the compounds which are stressed on the first syllable are the separable ones. To cite an example, *'abschreiben* and *'weitergehen* form the past tense *ich schrieb ab, ich ging weiter*; the past participle *abgeschrieben, weitergegangen* and the dependent infinitive *abzuschreiben, weiterzugehen*. The compounds which are not stressed on the first syllable are the nonseparable ones—*er'lauben, zer'stören* form the past *erlaubte, zerstörte*; the past participle *erlaubt, zerstört*; and the dependent infinitive *zu erlauben, zu zerstören*. In some cases the intonation alone indicates the difference between separable and nonseparable verbs with different meaning: *Ich möchte das Buch 'wieder holen* (primary stress on *wieder*: *I want to get the book again*). *Ich möchte das Buch wieder'holen* (primary stress on *holen*: *I want to review the book*). The different stresses indicate the different meanings and signal the fact that *'wieder holen* forms the past *holte wieder*, the past participle *wieder geholt* (*Ich holte das Buch wieder; Ich habe das Buch wieder geholt*), whereas *wieder'holen* is a nonseparable verb: *Ich wiederholte das Buch; Ich habe das Buch wiederholt*.

Learning the correct stress pattern of the verb (and every verb with its correct stress pattern) is thus not only a matter of correct intonation or stress but a necessity for correct grammatical usage and comprehension.

CHAPTER VI

Teaching Morphology

(A) GENERAL CONCEPTS

We have already defined morphemes as the smallest units of language that have a recognizable meaning or function of their own. For German, just as for English, it is useful to subdivide these units into three types:

1. The stems, or roots, of words.
2. The prefixes or suffixes that are used in the formation of words.
3. The morphemes that indicate the grammatical relationships.

Accordingly, in a word like *Vorstellung*, *Vor-* and *-ung* are morphemes of type 2, and *stell* represents type 1, a root. *Vor-* and *-ung* are reusable in words like *vor/dringen*, *vor/sichtig*, *Wiederhol/ung*, *Rett/ung*, whereas *stell* reappears in *Stell/e*, *ein/stell/en*. The word *einstellen* shows the example of a morpheme of type 3—the grammatical morpheme *-en* indicating the infinitive and reappearing in practically all infinitives of German: for example, *hol/en*, *sag/en*, *sprech/en*. The dividing line between the classes of morphemes is not necessarily sharp and unambiguous—that is, the *-er* of *Sprech/er* is a derivational morpheme indicating the name of agency, but it may also be considered grammatical in the sense that it is signaling a specific word class or case.

The morphemes posing the most serious problems to the student are the grammatical ones. Here we must note, first, that German, like English, has different types of grammatical morphemes. Some are endings, for instance, the plural morpheme *-er* of *Kind/er* (as the English *-s* or *-en* in *cats* or *oxen*). Other grammatical morphemes are expressed by changes **within** the stem, for example, in the alternation of the stem vowel in *geb* $\neq$ *gab*

85

(*ich gebe, ich gab*), the replacement of *e* by *a* is the morpheme indicating the past tense. (English uses this kind of grammatical morpheme quite frequently: *give* ≠ *gave*, *sing* ≠ *sang*.) A third type of grammatical morpheme—normally not found in English and therefore difficult for the student—is the "discontinuous" type: in the phrase *d/e/s Kind/es* both the ending of the article and the ending of the noun are part of the morpheme indicating the genitive, although they are separated by the noun. Yet to the speaker of German they both form part of a whole; omission of a part (*das Buch des *Kind*) will furnish a perhaps comprehensible but grammatically unacceptable expression.

As we stated earlier in this book, just as phonemes have their allophones so morphemes have their allomorphs, that is, their variations. All allomorphs of the same morpheme must fulfill two conditions: (1) They all must have the same meaning or function; (2) they must be in complementary distribution, that is, in the spot in which one of the variants occurs, another **cannot** occur.

Which variant or allomorph must be used is basically determined in two ways. One possibility is that the variant depends on the "phonetic environment," namely, the preceding or following sounds. Thus the ending of the masculine genitive "strong" declension is *-es* or *-s*: *des Wirtes*, *des Tag(e)s*; however, after noncompound words of more than one syllable only the *-s* ending is used: *des Vaters*, *des Hotels* (never **Vateres*). The other possibility is that the allomorph to be used is determined by the stem or word with which it combines. Accordingly, *der*, *die*, *das* are basically variants of the same morpheme, their choice being determined by the noun with which they are used. In a similar way the *-te* of *sagte* and the vowel change in *gab* (infinitive: *geben*) are variants of the same morpheme indicating the past tense: *sagen* requires the *-te* variant; *geben* requires the vowel change. These variations are, of course, basically unpredictable and constitute quite obviously one of the major headaches for the foreign language student and teacher. The possibility that variants of the same morpheme may be completely dissimilar must be reckoned with not only in the case of grammatical morphemes. It happens with root morphemes as well, though linguists like to classify this under the special category of **replacive**, or **suppletive**. The comparatives *besser* (of *gut*) or *mehr* (of *viel*) show root morphemes that have the same meaning as the one used in the positive but are completely different in form. The replacives also constitute an obvious teaching problem; fortunately there are few, and English and German are in general agreement in their use.

A list showing the combinations of a root morpheme with the grammatical morphemes with which it can possibly combine is called a **paradigm**. The list *give, gives, gave, giving, given* is the paradigm of the word *give* in English. In a language such as German, in which root morphemes can combine with various and unpredictable allomorphs of grammatical morphemes, the learning of paradigms, or at least partial paradigms, can be an important learning and teaching aid. However, one very essential fact must be kept in mind by the teacher as well as by the student, namely, that the paradigm by itself is a rather fortuitous and meaningless arrangement of words, unless the learning of each word in the paradigm is associated with its syntactical functioning in actual speech.

A short true experience may illustrate the point above. When I was eleven years old and a pupil in the fourth grade in Austria, formal German grammar was introduced to us in our native language, German. As part of this grammatical training, we had to learn the declension of the German noun. We received the grammatical explanation that the nominative is the case of actor, the accusative the case of the acted upon, the genitive the possessive case, and the dative the case of the indirect object. Next, we were asked to memorize paradigms: *der Vater, des Vaters, dem Vater, den Vater*. I remember quite vividly how some of my classmates and I stumbled over the sequence *dem Vater, des Vaters, der Vater*. When it came to the learning and recitation of the pronouns, the situation was even worse. One of my classmates, when asked to decline the pronoun *er*, produced quite proudly the rather remarkable sequence *er, seiner, *sir, sich* (on the analogy of *du, deiner, dir, dich*). Our teacher then had an inspiration! After all, he was not even teaching a foreign language! Why not rely on what we, as native speakers, knew anyway? He wrote four sentences on the board:

1. *Der Lehrer ist hier.*
2. *Ich lese das Buch des Lehrers.*
3. *Ich gehorche dem Lehrer.*
4. *Ich kenne den Lehrer.*

Afterward, he turned to the class and said: "You see, it is very simple. Any form that replaces *Lehrer* in sentence 1 is a nominative. A form replacing it in sentence 2 is a genitive, a replacement in sentence 3 is a dative, and a replacement in sentence 4 is an accusative." We had no more trouble with identifying cases, and forms like *sir disappeared from our repertory.

The teacher of German as a foreign language cannot rely on the student's ability to recognize nominative or genitive as forms that can replace other nominatives or genitives within the same construction; but the point is precisely that this is the ability he must create. *Der Vater, des Vaters, dem Vater, den Vater* is by itself a fortuitous jumble of forms. Unless we know into which "slots" of a sentence each form fits, it tells us very little about the grammar of German. Paradigms must be related to each other and to sentences. We can, for instance, relate paradigms to the sample sentences used in the paragraph above and write them next to each other:

der Vater	*die* Mutter	*das* Kind
des Vaters	*der* Mutter	*des* Kindes
dem Vater	*der* Mutter	*dem* Kind(e)
den Vater	*die* Mutter	*das* Kind

The vertical sequence in the chart, the **paradigmatic** arrangement, is accidental. Some textbooks prefer to put the accusative after the nominative or the genitive after the dative. What is real and represents the facts of German and the consciousness of the native speaker is shown in the horizontal columns, which express the syntactical, or **syntagmatic**, relationship: genitives can take the place of other genitives, datives can replace other datives. Instead of *Ich lese das Buch des Vaters*, we can say *Ich lese das Buch der Mutter* or *Ich lese das Buch des Kindes*; and *Ich gehorche dem Vater* can become *Ich gehorche der Mutter*, and so on.

German morphological variations must therefore be taught primarily as replacements of each other within the same syntactical construction. Paradigms, and especially the visual presentation of them, can be extremely useful provided that they are used to stress the syntactical functioning of the forms. In order to stress the basic fact that nominatives are replacements for each other just as genitives are replacements of other genitives, we have chosen the same underlining for different examples of the signals of the same cases: *nominative*, *genitive*, *dative*, *accusative*. For the purpose of illustration, we shall continue the practice of associating these underlinings with those cases in our discussion of noun, adjective, and pronoun morphology.

(B) MORPHOLOGY OF THE
NOUN, ADJECTIVE, AND PRONOUN

It is not our intention to give a total review or analysis of ⁀erman morphology in this book. Adequate descriptions of German morphology are found in various books (see Bibliography) and are implied in some form or other in any elementary German text. We shall be satisfied with pointing out some of the most important categories of German inflection and the teaching problems connected with them.

As far as the morphology of the German noun and adjective is concerned, it constitutes a problem principally in the area of the replacement operations. English nouns are inflected for number, but not for gender or case (except for the remnants of a possessive genitive: *my father's hat*). Thus the concepts of case and gender are rather strange and foreign to the speaker of English. In the case of determinors or adjectives, even the inflection for number is practically absent in English, except for a few remnants, such as **this** *book*, **these** *books*. This is just another way of saying that the speaker of English can, in his own language, take any singular or plural noun phrase in the form in which he remembers it and use it in a substitution operation to form a new sentence: for example, the noun phrase *this clever man* can be taken from the sentence *This clever man is here* and be used as a substitute in the sentence *I know that old woman* to form a new sentence, *I know this clever man*. The student who has learned the German equivalent of *this clever man* in the German sentence *Dieser kluge Mann ist hier* will tend to duplicate the English type of substitution operation. Substituting in—let us say—the sentence *Ich kenne diese alte Frau*, he will then arrive at *Ich kenne *dieser kluge Mann*. The job of the teacher is to make the student realize that the syntactic slot of *diese alte Frau* requires a different form, namely, *diesen klugen Mann*. But realization of what form is required is not enough. A great deal of practice is needed until the choice of the correct form becomes automatic.

The best way of dealing with the morphology of the German noun is first to involve the student in a great deal of substitution practice and then to resort to charts to systematize the student's knowledge. Finally, fluency is probably best achieved by a methodology that combines the use of charts with substitution in specific syntactic slots. As charts showing the main type of noun declension we suggest the following:

I. *Masculine*

		1.	2.	3.
sing.	Nom.	*der Mann*	*der Lehrer*	*der Tag*
	Gen.	*des Mannes*	*des Lehrers*	*des Tages*
	Dat.	*dem Mann(e)*	*dem Lehrer*	*dem Tag(e)*
	Acc.	*den Mann*	*den Lehrer*	*den Tag*
pl.	Nom.	*die Männer*	*die Lehrer*	*die Tage*
	Gen.	*der Männer*	*der Lehrer*	*der Tage*
	Dat.	*den Männern*	*den Lehrern*	*den Tagen*
	Acc.	*die Männer*	*die Lehrer*	*die Tage*

		4.	5.	6.
sing.	Nom.	*der Hase*	*der Mensch*	*der Staat*
	Gen.	*des Hasen*	*des Menschen*	*des Staates*
	Dat.	*dem Hasen*	*dem Menschen*	*dem Staate*
	Acc.	*den Hasen*	*den Menschen*	*den Staat*

pl.	Nom.	*die Hasen*	*die Menschen*	*die Staaten*
	Gen.	*der Hasen*	*der Menschen*	*der Staaten*
	Dat.	*den Hasen*	*den Menschen*	*den Staaten*
	Acc.	*die Hasen*	*die Menschen*	*die Staaten*

II. *Neuter*

		1.	2.	3.	4.
sing.	Nom.	*das Messer*	*das Meer*	*das Blatt*	*das Ohr*
	Gen.	*des Messers*	*des Meeres*	*des Blattes*	*des Ohres*
	Dat.	*dem Messer*	*dem Meere*	*dem Blatte*	*dem Ohre*
	Acc.	*das Messer*	*das Meer*	*das Blatt*	*das Ohr*
pl.	Nom.	*die Messer*	*die Meere*	*die Blätter*	*die Ohren*
	Gen.	*der Messer*	*der Meere*	*der Blätter*	*der Ohren*
	Dat.	*den Messern*	*den Meeren*	*den Blättern*	*den Ohren*
	Acc.	*die Messer*	*die Meere*	*die Blätter*	*die Ohren*

III. *Feminine*

		1.	2.	3.	4.
sing.	Nom.	*die Tochter*	*die Wand*	*die Sache*	*die Frau*
	Gen.	*der Tochter*	*der Wand*	*der Sache*	*der Frau*
	Dat.	*der Tochter*	*der Wand*	*der Sache*	*der Frau*
	Acc.	*die Tochter*	*die Wand*	*die Sache*	*die Frau*
pl.	Nom.	*die Töchter*	*die Wände*	*die Sachen*	*die Frauen*
	Gen.	*der Töchter*	*der Wände*	*der Sachen*	*der Frauen*
	Dat.	*den Töchtern*	*den Wänden*	*den Sachen*	*den Frauen*
	Acc.	*die Töchter*	*die Wände*	*die Sachen*	*die Frauen*

Note that on the charts we have drawn boxes, "blocking out" the weak ending -(*e*)*n*.

A series of nouns of the types mentioned in the charts above follows. The lists are merely examples and are not meant to be exhaustive. The symbol (··) indicates that the plural is formed with umlaut in the stem.

I. 1. *Wurm* (··), *Geist, Leib, Wald* (··)
   2. *Schüler, Apfel* (··), *Garten* (··)
   3. *Stein, Hut* (··), *Baum* (··)

     4. *Knabe, Bote, Affe*
     5. *Fürst, Held, Narr*
     6. *Mast, Schmerz, Doktor* (note plural *Dok'toren*)

II. 1. *Zeichen, Mädchen, Segel*
    2. *Pferd, Schiff, Gesetz, Geschäft*
    3. *Bad* (¨), *Band* (¨), *Glas* (¨), *Dorf* (¨), *Huhn* (¨), *Schwert, Weib*
    4. *Bett, Aug(e), Ende*

III. 1. *Mutter* (¨)
    2. *Bank* (¨), *Braut* (¨), *Gans* (¨), *Haut* (¨), *Luft* (¨)
    3 and 4. *Blume, Grenze, Grösse, Waage* (and most feminine nouns)

In connection with the charts, we should point out that it is also possible to restrict the underlining to the morphemes associated with a particular case, such as *des̲ Mann̲es̲*. From the linguistic point of view, this could be in a sense the correct procedure since only the *-es̲* and *-es̲* are to be associated with the genitive, whereas the *d-* and the *Mann* are really the root morphemes that reappear in *den Mann, die Männer*. However, for pedagogical reasons the underlining of the complete form seems preferable. The student must learn to retain complete units like *den Mann* or *des̲ Mann̲es̲* and cannot rely on composing them out of their morphemic constituents.

Charts of the type that have just been illustrated can be used only after the component elements have been introduced gradually in the context of speech and specific exercises. Extensive paradigmatic charts are not the starting point of instruction. As the elements composing the chart are introduced, they can be added to the chart until all types of nouns and all cases have been presented and practiced. As far as the order of presentation is concerned, two main strategies are possible: the teacher may attempt to introduce the four cases (singular and plural) all at once, or he may emphasize one case after the other, having one or several lessons dealing with the accusative, then several lessons with the dative, and so on. Since the substitution type of exercise deals always with replacement within the same case and since—as stated above—the "horizontal" relationships of the charts are the real ones, most linguists will prefer a course that introduces the forms by cases rather than by types of declension.

The substitution exercise dealing with cases can take two forms: either the substitution cue is given in the case that is required, or it is given in another case (usually the nominative) and the student has to provide the correct form himself.

TEACHER	STUDENT
Ich sehe das Kind.	*Ich sehe das Kind.*
_____ *den Mann.*	*Ich sehe den Mann.*

or

Ich sehe das Kind.	*Ich sehe das Kind.*
_____ *der Mann.*	*Ich sehe den Mann.*

The second type is obviously the more complicated exercise, since it presupposes a transformation into the required case by the student, and it will normally have to be prepared for by extensive practice in the first kind of substitution.

Once a declension chart (or at least a partial chart) has been developed, practice must switch back and forth between the learning of the endings and their syntactical application. This can be accomplished in various ways. The teacher can introduce model charts in the classroom and point to the forms on the chart as he (or the class) uses nouns or noun phrases in specific sentences. Or he can point to forms on the chart (*den Mann*, *den schönen Mann*) and then ask the student to provide sentences in which the forms are used (*Ich sehe den Mann*, *Ich kenne den Mann*). A homework assignment that can prove extremely helpful, if conscientiously done, consists of the following:

(a) The teacher suggests a series of sentence frames that are to be practiced during the week:

    1. *Der Lehrer ist hier.*
    2. *Ich kenne die Frau des Lehrers.*
    3. *Ich antworte dem Lehrer*
    4. *Ich sehe den Lehrer.*

(b) The student prepares on a sheet of paper a chart such as the following, showing the cases in singular and plural:

	Singular	*Plural*
Nom.		
Gen.		
Dat.		
Acc.		

(c) A series of nouns or noun phrases are assigned for practice during the week—for example, *die Frau, die Tochter; die junge Frau, die schöne Tochter, das kleine Kind*, and so on. The student then practices in the following manner: He might decide to practice *die schöne Tochter*. He closes his eyes and hits the chart with his pencil. If the pencil comes to rest in the area of the dative plural, he produces the sentence that requires the dative plural of the phrase: *Ich antworte den schönen Töchtern*. The student can then confirm the correctness of his answer by checking against a master chart; or he may consult the master chart if he is still uncertain about what the correct form should have been.

If he conscientiously practices for fifteen or thirty minutes all the nouns or noun phrases that have been assigned, he is bound to work up speed and learn how to use the forms in a syntactical context.

The article and the other limiting or determinative adjectives of German should always be practiced with the noun and presented in the charts followed by the nouns:

SINGULAR

	Masculine		Feminine	
Nom.	*dieser Mann*	*kein Mann*	*diese Frau*	*keine Frau*
Gen.	*dieses Mannes*	*keines Mannes*	*dieser Frau*	*keiner Frau*
Dat.	*diesem Mann*	*keinem Mann*	*dieser Frau*	*keiner Frau*
Acc.	*diesen Mann*	*keinen Mann*	*diese Frau*	*keine Frau*

Neuter

Nom.	*dieses Kind*	*kein Kind*
Gen.	*dieses Kindes*	*keines Kindes*
Dat.	*diesem Kind*	*keinem Kind*
Acc.	*dieses Kind*	*kein Kind*

PLURAL

Nom.	*diese Männer*	*keine Männer*
Gen.	*dieser Männer*	*keiner Männer*
Dat.	*diesen Männern*	*keinen Männern*
Acc.	*diese Männer*	*keine Männer*

After all the cases and forms have been learned, it will be helpful if the student realizes some of the characteristic features of the declension of the determinatives:

1. There is a group called the *der*-words, which take the endings of the definite article (*der, dieser, welcher, solcher, mancher*), and another group called the *ein*-words, which take the same endings as the indefinite article (*ein, kein*, and all the possessive adjectives, *mein, dein, sein, unser, euer, ihr*).

2. The difference between the *der*-words and the *ein*-words is that the latter have no ending in the masculine singular nominative, the neuter singular nominative, and the neuter singular accusative.

3. In the plural all determinatives, regardless of group or gender, take the same endings.

Connected with the declension of the limiting adjective, and to be taught in conjunction with it, is the morphology of the **descriptive adjective**. The morphology of the "normal" (descriptive) adjective offers the following problems:

1. In the predicate position it is used without ending (*Die Frau ist schön; Die Kinder sind schön*). The students may have a tendency to transfer this form without ending into the noun phrase—especially in the nominative. This tendency must be counteracted by practice that contrasts predicative and attributive use:

TEACHER	STUDENT
Ist die Frau schön?	*Ja, das ist eine schöne Frau.*
Ist das Kind schön?	*Ja, das ist ein schönes Kind.*

2. The student must learn the morphology involved in the comparison of the adjective:

dick	*dicker*	*am dicksten*	(*der dickste*)
gross	*grösser*	*am grössten*	(*der grösste*)
gut	*besser*	*am besten*	(*der beste*)
viel	*mehr*	*am meisten*	(*die meisten*)

The morphology of the comparative and superlative involves, in turn, several problems: some adjectives change their stem through umlaut in the comparative and superlative forms, some do not (*jung* ≠ *jünger*, but *dunkel/dunkler*). *Gut* and *viel* use replacives in the stem (*gut* ≠ *besser/am besten; viel* ≠ *mehr/am meisten*). The comparatives and superlatives can be used as descriptive adjectives in a noun phrase, such as *ein grösserer Mann, der grösste Mann*. Thus, the declensional endings of the adjective—to be discussed in the next paragraph—are, so to speak, superimposed on or added to the comparative and superlative endings. This amalgamation of two endings (-*er* + -*er* in *ein grösserer Mann*) is a fairly complicated process and is likely to give trouble to the student. It is therefore advisable to teach the comparative and superlative as part of the noun phrase only **after** the declension of the adjective as such has been completely mastered.

3. In the declension of the descriptive adjective as part of the noun phrase, the student must learn to distinguish the strong and the weak type of declension.

The endings of the strong type of declension are those of the *der*-words—except for the genitive singular of the masculine and neuter (*des Weines*, but *guten Weines*; *des Salzes*, but *guten Salzes*). Still it may be profitable to summarize the endings of the strong adjective declension as follows:

SINGULAR

	Masculine	*Feminine*	*Neuter*
Nom.	*guter Wein*	*gute Butter*	*gutes Gemüse*
Gen.	*guten Weines*	*guter Butter*	*guten Gemüses*
Dat.	*gutem Wein*	*guter Butter*	*gutem Gemüse*
Acc.	*guten Wein*	*gute Butter*	*gutes Gemüse*

PLURAL

Nom.	*gute Leute*
Gen.	*guter Leute*
Dat.	*guten Leuten*
Acc.	*gute Leute*

The use of the strong declension is in itself comparatively rare. It is used only when the adjective is not preceded by the limiting type of adjective. The use of nouns without limiting adjective in German parallels in most cases the speech habits of English. It will normally occur with proper names (*Heinrich ist hier/Henry is here*), names of countries (*Ich bin in Frankreich/I am in France*), the singular so-called "mass nouns" in the singular (*Ich trinke Milch/I drink milk*), and words indicating categories ("*Gattungsnamen*") in the plural (*Er hat viele Schüler*, = *He has many pupils*). The instances in which the genitive singular of the strong adjective declension may be used are rarer yet and are rapidly disappearing from spoken German; expressions such as *ein Krug guten Weines* or *ein Korb guten Gemüses* are considered old-fashioned. In actual speech they are replaced by a construction in which the noun expressing the material or substance agrees with the case of the noun expressing quantity: *Ich kaufe einen Krug guten Wein; Ich kaufe einen Korb gutes Gemüse; Das ist ein Glas kaltes Bier*. Thus, rather than belaboring the exceptions in which the strong adjective endings and the *der*-word endings do not agree, it may be preferable not to teach the genitive singular forms of the strong adjective declension at all.

4. The weak adjective declension is the one used after the limiting adjectives. Eventually, to summarize with a chart may be useful:

SINGULAR

	Masculine	Feminine	Neuter
Nom.	der gute Wein	die gute Butter	das gute Gemüse
	(ein guter Wein)		(ein gutes Gemüse)
Gen.	des guten Weines	der guten Butter	des guten Gemüses
Dat.	dem guten Wein	der guten Butter	dem guten Gemüse
Acc.	den guten Wein	die gute Butter	das gute Gemüse
			(ein gutes Gemüse)

PLURAL

Nom.	die guten Leute
Gen.	der guten Leute
Dat.	den guten Leuten
Acc.	die guten Leute

The salient feature of the weak declension may be summarized for the students as follows:

(a) The ending -en is used everywhere except (1) in all the nominatives of the singular and (2) in the accusative of the feminine and neuter singular.

(b) If ein-words rather than der-words are used, the endings of the der-words appear in the descriptive adjectives in those three cases in which the ein-words have no ending: in the masculine singular nominative, the neuter singular nominative, and the neuter singular accusative. Special practice may be needed to contrast the usage in those forms:

Ich sehe das schöne Kind.　but　Ich sehe ein schönes Kind.
Das schöne Kind ist hier.　but　Ein schönes Kind ist hier.
Der kluge Mann ist hier.　but　Ein kluger Mann ist hier.

This practice takes best the form of substitution exercises in which ein- and der-words are made to alternate:

Ich sehe das schöne Kind.
ein　　　Ich sehe ein schönes Kind.
dieses　Ich sehe dieses schöne Kind.
unser　 Ich sehe unser schönes Kind.

On the occasion of such exercises, it may be necessary to stress to the pupil that unser and euer are words ending in -er, but that they are ein-words, not der-words—that is, unser (in unser Kind) and ein (in ein Kind) have the same declensional ending, namely none.

Pronouns are all words that can replace a noun or a noun phrase. As far as the pronominal inflection of German is concerned, the demonstrative pronoun offers the least problem once the limiting adjectives have been mastered. The paradigm of the demonstrative pronoun *der* is practically the same as that of the limiting adjective, the demonstrative adjective, or the article: *Der Mann hat recht; Der hat recht; Ich kenne das Buch; Ich kenne das.* This pronominal use of *der*, *die* and *das* as accented replacements of the usually unstressed *er*, *sie*, *es* is an important feature of colloquial German, but it still is considered as substandard or vulgar by some people.

In the genitive the demonstrative pronouns are different from the article: singular masculine *dessen*, feminine *deren*, neuter *dessen;* plural *derer.* However, we should stress that we are dealing in the genitive with rare, as far as spoken German is concerned almost theoretical, forms. A genitive of a demonstrative pronoun would be used after certain verbs requiring the genitive (*bedürfen*, *gedenken*) and after some prepositions (*wegen*, *trotz*, *während*). Either usage is quite rare in spoken German: For example, *Ich erinnere mich dessen* or *Ich bedarf dessen* sounds stilted. Expressions like *wegen dessen* or *trotz dessen* are equally rare. One would rather say: *Ich erinnere mich daran*, or *trotzdem*, or *deshalb.* The other German demonstratives (*dieser*, *jener*) are declined as simple *der*-words, and the compound *derjenige* (used as the antecedent of a relative clause *derjenige welcher* . . .) is declined like *der* followed by a weak adjective. The relative pronouns *der* and *welcher* are declined like simple *der*-words. There are only two exceptions: (1) *welcher* cannot be used in the genitive; (2) the genitives of *der* are *dessen* (masc.), *deren* (fem.), and *dessen* (neut.) in the singular, and *deren* (masc., fem., neut.) in the plural.

In general it can be said that relative pronouns are not very frequent in spoken German and that especially the use of *welcher* as a relative pronoun is rare even in cultivated conversation. In written German both *der* and *welcher* are used abundantly.

The following chart summarizes the relative pronouns:

SINGULAR

	Masculine	Feminine	Neuter
Nom.	*der* (*welcher*)	*die* (*welche*)	*das* (*welches*)
Gen.	*dessen*	*deren*	*dessen*
Dat.	*dem* (*welchem*)	*der* (*welcher*)	*dem* (*welchem*)
Acc.	*den* (*welchen*)	*die* (*welche*)	*das* (*welches*)

PLURAL

Nom.	*die* (*welche*)
Gen.	*deren*
Dat.	*denen* (*welchen*)
Acc.	*die* (*welche*)

Practice of the relative pronouns must, of course, take the form of syntactical exercises in which sentences are combined:

Ich kenne die Frau. Die Frau ist nicht hier.
  Die Frau, die ich kenne, ist nicht hier.
Ich kenne den Mann. Der Mann ist nicht hier.
  Der Mann, den ich kenne, ist nicht hier.

or

Ich kenne das Kind der Frau. Die Frau ist nicht hier.
  Die Frau deren Kind ich kenne, ist nicht hier.
Ich kenne das Kind des Mannes. Der Mann ist nicht hier.
  Der Mann, dessen Kind ich kenne, ist nicht hier.

The possessive pronouns of German can be used in three variants, one without article, and two with articles:

Ist das Ihr Hut?   1.   *Ja, das ist meiner.*

2.   *Ja, das ist der meine.*

3.   *Ja, das ist der meinige.*

Variant 1 of the possessive pronoun corresponds simply to the possessive adjectives (*mein, dein, sein, unser, euer, ihr*), but with *-er* word ending:

Ist das mein Vater?   *Das ist meiner.*
Ist das meine Tüte?   *Ja, das ist meine.*
Ist das sein Kind?   *Ja, das ist seines.*

Variant 2 represents the possessive adjective preceded by the article: thus the possessive is declined according to the weak adjective declension. Variant 3 corresponds exactly to type 2: the definite article is used and the possessive takes the weak declension. However, the suffix *-ig* is added to the possessive stem: *mein, meinig; unser, unserig; ihr, ihrig.* Variants 2 and 3 are rarely used in conversational German, where they would be felt as having a stilted or perhaps humorous effect.

The interrogative pronouns are:

	Masculine	*Neuter*	
Nom.	*Wer*	*Was*	
Gen.	*Wessen*	(*wessen*)	
Dat.	*wem*		(*wo*)
Acc.	*wen*	*was*	(*wo*)

They are best studied in exercises in which the student is told to form questions for different parts of a sentence.

Der Schüler spricht mit dem Lehrer. *Wer spricht mit dem Lehrer?*
Mit wem spricht der Schüler?

Wer gibt Karl das Buch?
Robert gibt Karl das Buch. *Wem gibt Robert das Buch?*
Was gibt Robert Karl?

Particular care should be taken to point out to the student that, with certain prepositions, *wo* + preposition (*wor-* if the preposition begins with a vowel) combined into one word must be used rather than preposition + *was*. The latter usage is **sometimes** possible and occurs in colloquial German. Especially the use of *was* after prepositions requiring the accusative (*Über was redet er?*) is fairly widely accepted, although not yet official standard German. The author of the book remembers quite vividly the attempts made by his teachers to stamp out the use of preposition + *was* as unacceptable or substandard in his own speech. Thus:

Robert schreibt mit dem Bleistift. *Womit* (not **mit was*) *schreibt Robert?*

Robert freut sich über das Resultat. *Worüber freut sich Robert?*

It may also be necessary to point out to the student that—as in English *where(to)*—*wo*, *wohin*, may have to be used to ask for location and direction, rather than preposition + *was* (*what*).

Robert geht auf die Strasse. *Wohin* (not **auf was*) *geht Robert?*
Robert fährt auf der Strasse. *Wo fährt Robert?*

These examples also show the German compulsory distinction between direction and location (*wohin* vs. *wo*), a problem to which we shall briefly return in a different context (see Chapter 8).

The German reflexive and personal pronouns can be summarized in the following chart:

		1st Person	2nd Person	3rd Person		
sing.	Nom.	*Ich*	*du*	*er*	*sie*	*es*
	Gen.	*meiner*	*deiner*	*seiner*	*ihrer*	*seiner*
	Dat.	*mir*	*dir*	*ihm* (refl. *sich*)	*ihr* (*sich*)	*ihm* (*sich*)
	Acc.	*mich*	*dich*	*ihn* (refl. *sich*)	*sie* (*sich*)	*ihn* (*sich*)

		1st Person	2nd Person		3rd Person
pl.	Nom.	*wir*	*ihr*	*Sie*	*sie*
	Gen.	*unser*	*euer*	*Ihrer*	*ihrer*
	Dat.	*uns*	*euch*	*Ihnen* (*sich*)	*ihnen* (refl. *sich*)
	Acc.	*uns*	*euch*	*Sie* (*sich*)	*sie* (refl. *sich*)

There is thus no difference between the normal object pronoun and the reflexive use except in the third person, where for all datives and accusatives the reflexive uses the form *sich*: *Er schenkt K̲a̲r̲l̲ ein Buch, Er schenkt s̲i̲c̲h̲ ein Buch; Das freut s̲e̲i̲n̲e̲ M̲u̲t̲t̲e̲r̲, Er freut s̲i̲c̲h̲.* The English counterpart of the reflexive (*myself, yourself, himself*, etc.) is used not only reflexively (*He cut himself, Er hat sich geschnitten*), but also as an emphatic pronoun (*He did it himself*), in which case the German equivalent is not a reflexive, but rather the adverb or adjective *selbst* (*Er selbst hat es getan, Er hat es selbst getan*). German and English do not always overlap in the way in which reflexive actions are described. Thus German *Ich wasche mich*, may be rendered by English *I wash* (without *myself*). And German *Ich rasiere mich* corresponds normally to English *I shave*. Practice in the use of the reflexive forms and pronouns must therefore stress the areas in which English and German differ and must especially stress those German usages in which the corresponding English sentence would contain no reflexive construction whatsoever, for example, *Die Tür öffnete sich* ≠ *The door opened; Ich erhole mich* ≠ *I am recovering; Sie bewegt sich* ≠ *She is moving; Das hört sich gut an* or *Das lässt sich gut anhören* ≠ *That sounds pretty good*, and so forth.

The learning of the pronouns themselves is primarily a matter of combining the memorization of the forms with their continued use in replacement-type exercises:

Kennen Sie d̲e̲n̲ H̲e̲r̲r̲n̲?	*Ja, ich kenne i̲h̲n̲*
Kennen Sie d̲a̲s̲ B̲u̲c̲h̲?	*Ja, ich kenne e̲s̲.*
Kennen Sie d̲i̲e̲s̲e̲ S̲c̲h̲u̲l̲e̲?	*Ja, ich kenne s̲i̲e̲.*

Particular care must be taken to stress and practice the simple fact that German pronouns replace German grammatical gender. This may cause some difficulty to the student because English also distinguishes masculine, feminine, and neuter in the pronoun (*he, she, it*), but does not know grammatical gender and replaces with very minor exceptions (*the ship = she*), according to the sex of the noun that is referred to: (*The girl = she; The book = it, The man = he*).

In German, replacement according to sex is—at times—possible, especially if the antecedent is somewhat removed. Thus, after talking for a sentence or so about a girl (*das Mädchen*), the speaker of German is likely to refer to her as *she* (*sie*): *Ich habe das Mädchen vor zwei Wochen kennen gelernt. Es war wirklich bildhübsch. Und schöne Kleider hat **sie** gehabt.* However, in immediate replacement the grammatical gender is likely to take precedence and, of course, with all objects of feminine or masculine gender, replacement by gender is a must: *Wo ist der Tisch? Er ist im Garten. Wo liegt die Zeitung? Sie liegt auf dem Tisch.*

Before leaving the discussion of the salient points of the German declensional system, let us consider a final point not directly connected with the learning of the morphological forms as such. As we have stressed several times, the problem of the speaker of English is not only to learn the forms but also to learn the syntactical slot in which to use them. The subject of the sentence is always in the nominative, but the syntactical slot of the other cases is determined by the verb or preposition on which they depend. Even if the student remembers model sentences, replacement of verb or preposition in the model may change the case required in the dependent nouns. This means that the operation of verb substitution and preposition substitution must be drilled extensively in the learning of the declensional system. In order to reinforce the learning of prepositional and verb usage by visual memory, it is also advisable to use the visual symbols (underlining, color, etc.) associated with the specific cases in conjunction with the verbs and prepositions on which the cases depend.

Prepositions associated with the genitive:
während, wegen, trotz-statt, anstatt, diesseits, jenseits, oberhalb, unterhalb

Prepositions requiring the dative:
aus, ausser, bei, mit, nach, seit, von, zu, gegenüber, gemäss

Prepositions requiring the accusative:
durch, für, ohne, um, gegen, wider, bis

Prepositions requiring either the dative or the accusative:
an, auf, hinter, in, neben, über, unter, vor, zwischen

With the latter prepositions, the distinction between dative and accusative is primarily one between location and direction toward:

Er sitzt auf dem Sessel (where = wo)
but
Er legt das Buch auf den Sessel (where to = wohin)

In a similar way, visual aids may be used to reinforce the student's recollection of the case required by specific verbs.

Verbs requiring the genitive:
bedürfen, gedenken

Verbs requiring the dative:
gelingen, folgen, antworten, helfen, schaden, dienen, begegnen, danken, gehorchen

Verbs requiring the accusative:
This group is very large since it comprises all verbs which denote the idea of "making something" (for example, *machen, kochen, bauen*), and of "achieving a result" (*setzen, stellen, legen, tränken*). All the verbs beginning with the unseparable prefixes *be-, durch-, hinter-, über-, um-, un-*, take the accusative. (*beschreiben, beweisen, durchbrechen, übersetzen, unterstützen*). The majority of the impersonal verbs also take the accusative (for example, *es ärgert mich, es freut mich, es langweilt mich*). If verbs take objects in two different cases, this fact can also be indicated by using both types of visual aids:

Accusative + dative:
leihen, borgen, geben, liefern, reichen

Accusative + genitive:
berauben, anklagen, würdigen, sich bedienen

In the system used so far, we have utilized double underlining for the nominative. Since, however, the nominative can, by definition, not be used as object of a verb, we can utilize the double line to indicate that we are dealing with a verb which can have a double accusative object:

nennen, heissen, rufen, lehren, kosten

Visual aids (colors, underlinings) of the type suggested can be used effectively not only in the dictionary of a text but also with exercises and reading materials, until the case relationships have impressed themselves upon the student:

Ich lege das Buch auf den Tisch.
Ich spreche mit meinem Freund.
Ich gebe meinem Freund das Buch.
Ich nannte meinen Freund unseren Leiter.
Ich klagte ihn des Diebstahls an.
Wir gehorchen unseren Eltern.

As the student progresses and gets more and more practice in developing the concepts of case and case relationship, the visual aids must be—gradually—withdrawn so that he learns to operate quickly and efficiently without the crutches of visual aids. But even long after the aids are withdrawn, the visual memory of *durch* or *helfen*, as opposed to *durch* (*?*), *helfen* (*?*), may make the difference between the choice of a correct or incorrect form.

(C) MORPHOLOGY OF THE VERB

Just as in noun morphology, the presentation of paradigms and their learning has been part of German verb teaching for a long time. Many textbooks require of the student to memorize, if not the total paradigm, at least the basic forms from which others can be derived:

> *sagen, sagst, sagte, gesagt* or *geben, gibst, gab, gegeben.*

Another practice followed by many teachers is to have the student conjugate verbs, for instance, *ich spreche, du sprichst, er spricht, wir sprechen, ihr sprecht, sie sprechen.* As in the case of noun paradigms, we want to emphasize that there is nothing wrong with learning arrangements of forms, provided that they are related to actual practice with real language. As a matter of fact, the memorization of base forms like *geben, gibst, gab, gegeben* may prove extremely helpful, and as far as conjugating verbs is concerned, it is obvious that even in isolation it is a far more useful exercise than the declining of nouns. *Ich spreche, du sprichst, er spricht* are a series of utterances that can occur either by themselves or as syntactical segments of larger units. The main pedagogical objection against overdoing the conjugation drills is probably that the utterances are always spoken in the same grammatical *ich, du, er, sie, es, wir, ihr, sie* sequence. The result may be that a response like *sie geben* becomes tied to the preceding *ihr gebt*. Thus the student may have to recite the entire conjugation in order to get to the third person plural. The situation is not unlike the one represented by the person who has to recite an entire poem in order to quote a line toward the end. This situation can be avoided by giving practice in producing sentences in which the personal pronouns are used as cues and in which the sequence of persons is jumbled up:

TEACHER:	STUDENT:
Ich spreche Deutsch.	*Ich spreche Deutsch.*
Karl _____ .	*Karl spricht Deutsch.*
Sie _____ .	*Sie sprechen Deutsch.*

Charts of the type presented below will be helpful to the student. Initial presentation of material should emphasize the **syntactical** rather than the **paradigmatic** relationship; in other words, first-person forms are to be associated with other first-person forms which can replace them in the sentence.

The German verb is best analyzed as being composed of a stem (such as *sag*) and a set of endings (such as *-en* for the infinitive). The present tense is derived from the stem and the set of endings shown in the chart below:

$\boxed{ich}$ sag $\boxed{e}$	$\boxed{wir}$ sag $\boxed{en}$ *
$\boxed{du}$ sag $\boxed{st}$ *	$\boxed{ihr}$ sag $\boxed{t}$ *
$\boxed{er}$ sag $\boxed{t}$ *	$\boxed{sie}$ sag $\boxed{en}$ *

Thus the first and third person plural are normally identical with the infinitive.

The following exceptions exist to the formation of the present tense as illustrated above:

1. A series of verbs, the so-called modal auxiliaries (*dürfen, können, sollen, wollen, müssen, mögen*), and the verb *wissen* do not take a third person singular ending (as *shall, will, can, must, may, ought* in English do not take *-s* in the third person).

2. Some verbs—all of them so-called strong verbs, which form their past by a change in the stem vowel—change their stem vowel also in the present second and third person singular, for example, *ich schlage, du schlägst, er schlägt, wir schlagen, ihr schlagt, sie schlagen*. This irregularity must be learned by including the second person singular with the base forms to be remembered.

3. The auxiliary verbs (auxiliary because they are used in the syntactical formation of other tenses) have irregular present tenses: *haben* and *werden* are irregular only in the singular (*ich habe, du hast, er hat, ich werde, du wirst, er wird*). *Sein* is irregular throughout (*ich bin, du bist, er ist, wir sind, ihr seid, sie sind*).

Basically the past tense of German is derived in two ways: (1) the majority of verbs form a past stem by adding *-te* to the stem of the verb. These verbs are classified as weak verbs. (2) A large number of verbs form their past stem by a change in the stem vowel. These are the so-called strong verbs. Both types of verbs then add to the stem the person indicators—which are the same as in the present tense—except for the first and third person singular in which no person indicator is added.

* The above-mentioned endings have the following variants: *n* for *en* if the last syllable of the stem contains /ə/: *wunder(n)*; *t* for *st* if the stem ends in /s/, /z/: *du liest, du weisst*; *est* or *et* for *st* or *t* if the stem ends in /t/, /d/ or /n/: *du wendest, er wendet, es regnet*.

The past tense of a weak verb, for instance, *sagen*, is thus the following:

(ich) sag|te|○   (wir) sag|te|(n)
(du) sag|te|(st)   (ihr) sag|te|(t)
(er) sag|te|○   (sie) sag|te|(n)

Note that in the description above, the morpheme denoting past tense is indicated by a box ☐, whereas the circle ○ is used for the person indicator. With a strong verb the morpheme (allomorph) denoting the past is, of course, the change in the stem vowel:

(ich) g|a|b○   (wir) g|a|b(en)
(du) g|a|b(st)   (ihr) g|a|b(t)
(er) g|a|b○   (sie) g|a|b(en)

In addition to strong and weak verbs, German has also a limited number of verbs that are classed as irregular, or "mixed." These are the words in which the allomorph indicating past tense is signaled by both the *-te* suffix and the change in the vowel, for example, the past form of *nennen*:

(ich) n|a|nn|te|○   (wir) n|a|nn|te|(n)
(du) n|a|nn|te|(st)   (ihr) n|a|nn|te|(t)
(er) n|a|nn|te|○   (sie) n|a|nn|te|(n)

Words belonging in this category are *brennen, rennen, kennen, senden, wenden, wissen, denken,* and, among the modal auxiliaries, *müssen, können, dürfen,* and *mögen.*

The auxiliary verbs *haben, sein, werden* form irregular stems (*hatte, war, wurde*) that, however, combine with the regularly used person indicators (—, st, —, -en, -t, -en).

German has two subjunctives. Both use the same person markers (-e, -est, -e, -en, -et, -en), but they add these markers to different stems. The subjunctive I adds these markers to the present-tense stem, the subjunctive II is formed by adding these markers to the past stem.

Subjunctive I		Subjunctive II	
(ich) sag(e)　(wir) sag(en)		(ich) sag|t|(e)　(wir) sag|t|(en)	
(du) sag(est)　(ihr) sag(et)		(du) sag|t|(est)　(ihr) sag|t|(et)	
(er) sag(e)　(sie) sag(en)		(er) sag|t|(e)　(sie) sag|t|(en)	
(ich) geb(e)　(wir) geb(en)		(ich) g|ä|b(e)　(wir) g|ä|b(en)	
(du) geb(est)　(ihr) geb(et)		(du) g|ä|b(est)　(ihr) g|ä|b(et)	
(er) geb(e)　(sie) geb(en)		(er) g|ä|b(e)　(sie) g|ä|b(en)	

In connection with the formation of the subjunctive, the following other rules, or exceptions, may be noted:

1. In the subjuncitve I the verbs *sein* and *wissen* form irregular subjunctives (*sei, seiest, sei, seien, seiet, sein; wisse, wissest,* and so on).

2. With regular weak verbs the past tense and the subjunctive II are identical.

3. The subjunctive II of strong verbs, although based on the past stem, frequently includes an umlaut in the stem.

4. Some strong verbs form an irregular subjunctive II in the sense that the stem vowel cannot be derived from the past tense, for example:

Infinitive	Past Tense	Subjunctive II
sterben	starb	stürbe
werfen	warf	würfe
stehen	stand	stünde

5. The mixed verbs which have an *e* in the present stem use *e* (not *a*, or *ä*) in the subjunctive II: *brennen*, past tense *brannte;* subjunctive II *brennte. Nennen, kennen, senden* (subj. II *sendete*), *wenden* (subj. II *wendete*) follow the same pattern. In actual practice the subjunctive forms *brennte, sendete, wendete* are used so rarely that they would strike most Germans as odd or perhaps even "wrong." *Denken, wissen, bringen* use the past stem with umlaut:

Infinitive	Past Tense	Subjunctive II
denken	dachte	dächte
wissen	wusste	wüsste
bringen	brachte	brächte

6. The modal auxiliaries *müssen, können, dürfen, mögen* and the auxiliary verbs *haben, sein, werden* form the subjunctive II with umlaut:

Infinitive	Past Tense	Subjunctive II
müssen	musste	müsste
können	konnte	könnte
mögen	mochte	möchte
sein	war	wäre
haben	hatte	hätte
werden	wurde	würde

7. The modals *sollen* and *wollen* form their subjunctives II regularly with their past tenses *sollte, wollte.*

The actual use of the subjunctive is a matter of syntax (we shall return to it in Chapter 8). Like all other forms of the verb, the subjunctive should be practiced in a syntactical context. One of the uses of the subjunctive is its employment in indirect discourse in standard literary German. Therefore a good way of practicing it is in transformation exercises from direct to indirect speech:

> *Er ist krank. Er sagt, dass er krank sei.*
> *Er sagt, er sei krank.*
>
> or
>
> *Er sagt, dass er krank wäre.*
> *Er sagt, er wäre krank.*

Other inflected forms of German include the various imperatives. They may be classified as follows:

1. The *Sie* and *wir* imperatives are identical with the present tense (except for the post position of the pronouns):

> *Gehen wir nach Hause!*
> *Gehen Sie nach Hause!*

2. The *ihr* imperative (second person plural) is identical with the second person plural, but used without pronoun:

> *Geht nach Hause!*

3. The third person singular imperative, used primarily in a few fixed expressions, is identical with the present subjunctive:

> *Er lebe hoch!*

4. The second person singular imperative is the only one which involves a new form to be learned. It is normally identical with the stem + *e*: *geh(en)/gehe*, *sag(en)/sage* (in colloquial German the *e* is often dropped). With strong verbs that have an *e* in the present stem and replace it by *i* or *ie* in the second person singular, the imperative also takes *i* or *ie* in the stem:

> *sehen/du siehst;* imperative: *sieh!*
> *vergessen/du vergisst;* imperative: *vergiss!*
> *geben/du gibst;* imperative: *gib!*

The German verb also has three forms that are not conjugated for number or person (in other words, are not **finite**) namely, the infinitive (stem + *en*: *sagen*, *sprechen*), the present participle (infinitive + *d*: *sagend*, *sprechend*; exception *seiend*), and the past participle. The past participle is formed by the prefix *ge-* and the suffix *-t* in case of weak verbs:

sag(en)/(ge)sag(t), and by the prefix *ge-*, the suffix *-en*, and a possible stem change in the case of strong verbs: *sing(en)/(ge)s(u)ng(en)*; *sprech(en)/ (ge)spr(o)ch(en)*. The formation of the past participle is further complicated by the fact that verbs with so-called separable prefixes (primary accent on the prefix) retain the prefix before the *ge-*: *anstell(en)/an(ge)-stell(t)*; *vorstell(en)/vor(ge)stell(t)*. Words with inseparable prefixes and words ending in *-ieren* (originally foreign borrowings) do not use the *ge-* prefix: *verkehr(en)/verkehr(t)*, *belehren/belehr(t)*, *spazier(en)/spazier(t)*, *amüsier(en)/amüsier(t)*.

Some usages of the participle will be discussed briefly in Chapter 8. It is important, however, to remember that in German the usage of the present participle is far more restricted than that of its English counterpart (the *-ing* form):

I am working.	*Ich arbeite.*
Working is good for you.	*Arbeiten ist gut für Sie.*
He started working.	*Er fing an zu arbeiten.*
Without working you won't succeed.	*Ohne zu arbeiten werden Sie keinen Erfolg haben.*

Therefore it seems advisable to introduce the present participle **late** in the course, after the correct German usages (simple present tense, infinitives as nouns or after verbs and preposition) have been firmly established.

The main use of the past participle is in the formation of the compound tenses; the main problem is the learning of the strong past participles in particular and of the strong verb conjugation in general. Most textbooks present the verb according to certain groups, usually according to the stem vowels in the infinitive, the second person singular present, the past tense, and the past participle. We shall very briefly present a model of such a grouping, without trying to be exhaustive:

I.	ei, ei, ie, ie:	*schr(ei)ben, schr(ei)bst, schr(ie)b, geschr(ie)ben* (*schweigen, steigen, treiben, verzeihen*)
II.	ei, ei, i, i:	*schn(ei)den, schn(ei)dest, schn(i)tt, geschn(i)tten* (*beissen, leiden, reiten*)
III.	ie, ie, o, o:	*b(ie)gen, b(ie)gst, b(o)g, geb(o)gen* (*fliessen, fliegen, verbieten, verlieren*)
IV.	i, i, a, u:	*b(i)nden, b(i)ndest, b(a)nd, geb(u)nden* (*finden, singen, springen, trinken*)
V.	i, i, a, o:	*gew(i)nnen, gew(i)nnst, gew(a)nn, gew(o)nnen*
VI.	e, i, a, o:	*br(e)chen, br(i)chst, br(a)ch, gebr(o)chen* (*werfen, gelten, helfen, sprechen*)

VII.	e, i(e), ä, e:	*g(e)ben, g(i)bst, g(a)b, geg(e)ben*
		(*essen, lesen, sehen, vergessen*)
VIII.	e, e, o, o:	*h(e)ben, h(e)bst, h(o)b, geh(o)ben*
		(*weben, melken*)
IX.	1. e, i, o, o:	*f(e)chten, f(i)chst, f(o)chte, gef(o)chten*
		(*schwellen, schmelzen*)
	2. ä, ä, o, o:	*erw(ä)gen, erw(ä)gst, erw(o)g, erw(o)gen*
X.	1. a, ä, u, a:	*f(a)hren, f(ä)hrst, f(u)hr, gef(a)hren*
		(*graben, schlagen, tragen, waschen, wachsen*)
	2. a, a, u, a:	*sch(a)ffen, sch(a)ffst, sch(u)f, gesch(a)ffen*
XI.	1. a, ä, ie, a:	*f(a)llen, f(ä)llst, f(ie)l, gef(a)llen*
		(*behalten, lassen, raten, schlafen*)
	2. a, ä, i, a:	*f(a)ngen, f(ä)ngst, f(i)ng, gef(a)ngen*
	3. au, äu, ie, au:	*l(au)fen, l(aü)fst, l(ie)f, gel(au)fen*
XII.	ei, ei, ie, ei:	*h(ei)ssen, h(ei)sst, h(ie)ss, geh(ei)ssen*
XIII.	u, u, ie, u:	*r(u)fen, r(u)fst, r(ie)f, ger(u)fen.*

In addition to these groups of strong verbs, the student must learn to master the irregular and mixed groups. We shall briefly enumerate the irregular and mixed verbs.

MIXED VERBS

Infinitive	*Second Person Present*	*Past*	*Past Participle*
denken	*denkst*	*dachte*	*gedacht*
brennen	*brennst*	*brannte*	*gebrannt*
kennen	*kennst*	*kannte*	*gekannt*
nennen	*nennst*	*nannte*	*genannt*
rennen	*rennst*	*rannte*	*gerannt*
senden	*sendest*	*sandte*	*gesandt*
wenden	*wendest*	*wandte*	*gewandt*
bringen	*bringst*	*brachte*	*gebracht*
wissen	*weisst*	*wusste*	*gewusst*

All of these strong, mixed, and irregular verbs add up to a rather bewildering array of forms to which the pupil must be introduced gradually, but which cannot be mastered except by continuous practice and a certain amount of sheer role memorization of base forms. The wise teacher will make a judicious choice of irregular and strong verbs and insist that the pupil learn well a limited number of frequently used verbs

IRREGULAR VERBS

Infinitive	Second Person Present	Past	Past Participle
This group includes the auxiliary verbs:			
haben	*hast*	*hatte*	*gehabt*
sein	*bist*	*war*	*gewesen*
werden	*wirst*	*wurde*	*geworden*
and those which deviate from the pattern of the normal **weak**,			
strong, or **mixed** types:			
stehen	*stehst*	*stand*	*gestanden*
gehen	*gehst*	*ging*	*gegangen*
sitzen	*sitzt*	*sass*	*gesessen*
besitzen	*besitzt*	*besass*	*besessen*
legen	*legst*	*lag*	*gelegen*
bekommen	*bekommst*	*bekam*	*bekommen*
stossen	*stösst*	*stiess*	*gestossen*
tun	*tust*	*tat*	*getan*

rather than try to force him to retain a large number of comparatively rare forms.

The following device can enable the student to train himself in the formation of verb forms. He makes a grid which shows to the left the personal pronouns and at the top the names of the tenses: Present, Past. Other tenses may be added as the student learns them. (Although their formation is really a syntactical problem and to be discussed later, the use of the tenses implies practice in the morphology of the auxiliary verbs, the infinitives, past participles, and so forth).

Pronoun	Present			Past			Perfect	Pluperfect	Future
ich									
du	1	2	3						
er									
wir				1	2	3			
ihr									
sie									

A series of short sentences can be assigned as practice for the week, such as:

1. *Ich spreche mit meinem Freund.*
2. *Ich denke an meine Mutter.*

The student is then asked to practice in the following manner: He closes his eyes and hits the grid at random with his pencil. He opens his eyes and sees on what square his pencil has come to rest. Then he produces as quickly as possible the sentence that corresponds to the particular square of the Past column, the student has cued himself for the sentence, practicing with sentence 1 of his assignment and his pencil has hit the *wir* square of the Past column, the student has cued himself for the sentence, *Wir sprachen mit unserem Freund.* If he is uncertain about his answer or cannot supply one, he can check the answer by consulting the textbook— or better yet, he can write out (or the teacher can prepare for him) a sample chart showing the correct answers for at least some sentences. The sample chart can then be used for checking the student's responses (thus reinforcing correct answers and suggesting additional practice if the correct answers are not forthcoming). Aside from affording practice in the morphology of the verb, this type of chart can also be used for elementary syntactical training. Various complications of a syntactical nature can be added; for example, as we have indicated, **each** square of the chart can be divided into several parts: If the student's pencil hits part 1, the positive form of the verb is required; hitting part 2 requires transformation into the negative; hitting part 3 calls for the interrogative form. Thus, still thinking in terms of practice sentence 1 (*Ich spreche mit meinem Freund*), a "hit" into section 2 of the *wir* square of the Perfect column requires the response, *Wir haben mit unserem Freund nicht gesprochen.*

(D) WORD FORMATION

In addition to stem and grammatical endings, German has a large number of morphemes used in word derivation. Actually the difference between derivational morphemes and grammatical morphemes is **not** really very obvious and clear-cut: The ending -*en* of the infinitives is certainly a grammatical morpheme; but since it is used to produce a verb like *sprechen* from a stem (for example, *Sprech-* as in *Sprech/er*), why call it "grammatical" and the ending -*er*, used to produce a noun from the same stem, "derivational"? Actually the main difference between grammatical and derivational morphemes seems to be as follows: (1) the meaning of "grammatical morpheme" is more constant and better defined, and (2) the use of grammatical morphemes is more highly predictable. In other words, all infinitives end in -en, and verb stem + en always means "infinitive." But let us look at a derivational morpheme such as -ling. Some adjectives, for instance, *feig* and *jung*, can be transformed into nouns by adding this suffix: *Feigling, Jüngling;* -ling seems to have the meaning of "person having the quality of . . ." The same transformation applied to *früh* gives the noun *Frühling* (*spring*); and applied to the adjective *alt*, it furnishes **Ältling*—a nonexistent word (that will probably impress the native speaker as an attempt to be funny).

Nevertheless, learning the main derivational suffixes and prefixes of German will prove a tremendous help to the student. It will certainly increase his passive vocabulary significantly because it will afford the possibility of inferring the meaning of many words. A student who knows, for example, the word *verwandt* and the general meaning of the suffix -schaft can guess the meaning of *Verwandtschaft*. The student who has grasped the general usage of the suffixes -keit and -heit and who knows the meaning of *klug* or *tapfer* can infer *Tapferkeit* and *Klugheit*.

An additional advantage comes from familiarity with the derivational ending. In the case of the nouns the endings are almost without exception associated with a particular gender. Making the student aware of the meaning as well as the gender implied by the derivational suffix can also contribute to grammatical correctness.

The exercises used in teaching derivational morphemes can be of two types: one type consists of emphasizing passive recognition. In other words, the student may be asked to keep lists of words (preferably each with a sample sentence), using the same derivational morphemes. As he progresses with his German course, he accumulates word lists of nouns ending in -schaft, -tum, -heit, and forms a concept of the meaning of those derivational suffixes. The other type of exercise consists of giving practice in active word formation. The student may be given a model sentence of the type *Der Arbeiter arbeitet;* then he is asked to form parallel sentences with verbs, such as *rauben, mördern, dienen: Der Räuber raubt*, and so forth. Or the student may receive the explanation of the meaning of a suffix, for example, the suffix -ung indicates an action or its result. Then he is asked to rewrite sentences, using nouns ending in -ung: *Die, die uns regieren haben recht* (*Die Regierung hat recht*); *Ich wohne im dritten Bezirk* (*Meine Wohnung ist im dritten Bezirk*). This active type of exercise is also very valuable. However, it is important to impress upon the student that the transformation operation involved in the exercise can be applied by him only to the restricted number of examples given in the exercise itself. This is usually **not** the case in the grammatical type of transformation exercise. There is, therefore, the danger that the active type of word-formation exercise may encourage the creation of unacceptable and impossible words on the part of the student.

We list—with examples—**some** of the most important morphemes used in the formation of nouns:

Masculine Nouns

-er	nouns of agency	*Sprecher, Jäger, Fleischer, Bäcker*
-ler	nouns of agency	*Tischler, Künstler*
-ner	nouns of agency	*Redner, Lügner*
-el	means, tools	*Schlüssel, Gürtel, Hebel, Flügel* (Note, however, *das Segel, der Würfel*)
-rich		*Fähnrich, Wüterich*
-ling		*Jüngling, Frühling, Säugling*

Feminine Nouns

-e	abstract quality	*Grösse, Liebe, Höhe, Lüge*
-ei	store; action (with derogatory connotation)	*Bäckerei, Tischlerei, Spielerei, Schmeichlerei*
-ung	action; result of an action	*Zeichnung, Handlung, Erfindung, Bewasserung*
-schaft	relationship; collectivity	*Knechtschaft, Burschenschaft Freundschaft, Liebschaft*
-er + in	noun of agency	*Müllerin, Bäckerin, Meisterin*
-heit	collectivity	*Menschheit, Gütigkeit, Reinheit,*
-keit	abstract quality	*Fröhlichkeit*

Neuter Nouns

-tum	quality; collectivity	*Reichtum, Christentum, Judentum, Fürstentum*
-chen	diminutive	*Mädchen, Körbchen, Hündchen*
-lein	diminutive	*Büchlein, Vöglein*
-nis		*Zeugnis, Bedürfnis, Gefängnis*
-sal		*Schicksal, Drangsal*
-sel		*Rätsel*
Ge-	generic terms	*Gehör, Gemüse, Gedicht, Gefälle* (Note, however, *der Geruch, die Geschichte,* etc.)

Adjectives have also various characteristic derivational endings, mostly with the meaning of "full of" or "quality of." The student should recognize these endings, but should be warned not to form his own words or confuse derivational suffixes.

-voll		*gefahr**voll**, macht**voll***
-ig		*mut**ig**, salz**ig**, richt**ig***
-lich		*kind**lich**, lächer**lich**, wesent**lich**, schmerz**lich**, töd**lich***
-isch		*neid**isch**, kind**isch**, französ**isch**, russ**isch**, jüd**isch***
-bar		*frucht**bar**, ehr**bar**, dank**bar**, ess**bar**, heil**bar***
-sam		*furcht**sam**, spar**sam**, arbeit**sam***
-haft		*fehler**haft**, mangel**haft***
-los	without	*fehler**los**, arbeits**los**, gefahr**los**, mitte**llos***
-en	made of	*gold**en***
un-	negative prefix	***un**verständlich, **un**begreiflich, **un**dankbar, **un**gesund*
miss-	negative prefix	***miss**verständlich, **miss**vergnügt*

Most of the prefixes used in the formation of verbs carry the meaning of finishing or perfecting the action. As a matter of fact, the prefix *ge-*, which has become generalized as the prefix used in the formation of the past participle, is just one of various prefixes indicating completion of the action.

er-		***er**weichen, **er**holen, **er**hitzen, **er**halten, **er**bleichen*
ver-		***ver**stehen, **ver**derben, **ver**danken, **ver**jagen, **ver**gessen (Note the negative aspect of *ver-* in ***ver**ziehen, **ver**derben, **ver**wechseln, **ver**gessen, **ver**werfen)*
zer-		***zer**reissen, **zer**stören, **zer**schneiden*
ge-		***ge**hören, **ge**brauchen, **ge**niessen, **ge**lingen, **ge**schehen*
be-		***be**ruhigen, **be**wässern, **be**setzen, **be**trauern*
-eln	diminutive action	*läch**eln**, streich**eln**, säus**eln**, kling**eln** (Note that the *-n* is a variant of the *-en* morpheme of the infinitive: lächeln/past tense *lächel-te*)*

Quite often a series of derivative morphemes may be used to form a word, for example, *dank/en   dank/bar   un/dank/bar   Un/dank/bar/keit; steig/en   be/steig/en   be/steig/bar   un/be/steig/bar   Un/be/steig/bar/keit;*

em/pfind/en   em/pfind/lich   un/em/pfind/lich   Un/em/pfind/lich/keit;
Arbeit   arbeits/los   Arbeits/los/ig/keit;
stech/en   be/stech/en   be/stech/lich   Un/be/stech/lich/keit.

From the careful inspection of series in which words are successively transformed into new words by the successive addition of derivational morphemes, it is possible to arrive at certain generalizations about German word formation. The existence, for instance, of an adjective ending in -*lich* seems to assure the possibility of deriving from the adjective a noun ending in -*keit*. As of now, no thorough study of the transformational rules of German word formation is available. Therefore it does not seem possible or profitable to teach the process of word formation as such. Rather, it seems advisable to spend some time with the analysis of long compounds and words containing several derivational morphemes to make clear to the student how he can infer the meaning of such words as *Arbeitslosenunterstützung* from his knowledge of the words *Arbeit* and *unterstützen* and the derivational morphemes involved. The student could then be asked to go through exercises that consist of his deducing the meaning of words from the stem, the derivational morphemes, and the context; for instance, students knowing the words *Arbeit* and *unterstützen* and the derivational morphemes could be asked to supply the meaning of the underlined word in this sentence:

Karls Familie hatte Hunger, weil Karl keine <u>Arbeitslosenunterstützung</u>
   erhielt.
Or (on the basis of knowing *taugen*) they could be asked for the meaning of the word *Untauglichkeit* in the sentence:
Infolge seiner <u>Untauglichkeit</u> zum Militärdienst konnte Karl nicht Soldat
   werden.

CHAPTER VII

Teaching Syntactical Patterns

(A) WORD ORDER

German word order is one of the major problems for the student. The reasons are obvious, although German word order corresponds in some instances to English word order:

> ^{1}*Karl* ^{2}*sieht* ^{3}*den* ^{4}*Jungen.*
> ^{1}*Charles* ^{2}*sees* ^{3}*the* ^{4}*boy.*

It clashes in other cases:

> ^{1}*Karl* ^{2}*hat* ^{3}*den* ^{4}*Jungen* ^{5}*gesehen.*
> ^{1}*Charles* ^{2}*has* ^{5}*seen* ^{3}*the* ^{4}*boy.*

In addition, German word order combines flexibility and rigidity in a rather complicated fashion: *Karl hat immer mit seinem Freund gesprochen; Mit seinem Freund hat Karl immer gesprochen; Karl hat mit seinem Freund immer gesprochen*—even *Gesprochen hat Karl mit seinem Freund immer*, are all possible sentences. **Hat gesprochen Karl mit seinem Freund*, or *Karl mit seinem . . .* are **not** possible. This choice within a rigid frame makes word order probably even more difficult and bewildering than absolute rigidity by itself is likely to be. Just what determines the choices within the rigid frame is perhaps one of the most interesting problems of research in German syntax. In our discussion, which is concerned with the teaching problems on the elementary level, we shall however emphasize the rigid frame rather than the more subtle differences expressed by the freedom within this rigid structure. German word order is generally described by various formulas specifying the possible sequence of syntactical elements. Since our primary concern is with the teaching rather than the description of German, we shall not reproduce these formulas here. Valuable as they may be for the description of the language, they are likely to be too complex to furnish the student a guide for the process of creating German sentences. We shall rather attempt to describe the teaching strategy that can be employed in approaching German word order.

For the student, the German syntax should be developed from a small nucleus sentence or sentence-type and gradually be expanded. Let us give a possible example. (In our example we shall use different types of underlining to distinguish different segments of the sentence. If the teacher has used underlining to illustrate case relationships, it is preferable to use different symbols for the segments of the sentence. The use of different colors is also very effective. In general the complexity of German morphology and syntax makes the use of visual cues desirable, especially when more complicated structures are introduced.)

1. We start with the small sentence-type subject + finite verb: *Karl arbeitet*. Since the sequence *Karl arbeitet* corresponds exactly to the English word order of subject + verb, many teachers may want to introduce some adverbial modifiers at this early point in the course, for example, *heute arbeitet Karl* or *Karl arbeitet heute*, in order to keep the student from overlearning a German-English correspondence that he will have to abandon in many instances. At any rate, the student must learn that in any German main clause, subject + finite verb (the verb that is inflected for person and number) are usually next to each other and inseparable. Compare this with English: *Charles finally arrived in New York; Charles always knows the truth.*

2. The next step may be to expand the verb into a predicate consisting of a finite verb and some other element.

> *Karl arbeitet. Karl hat gearbeitet.*
> *Karl arbeitet. Karl will arbeiten.*
> *Karl ist intelligent.*
> *Karl ist Student.*
> *Karl bleibt ruhig.*

3. Then the student must learn that other elements of the sentence to be added become enclosed by the finite verb and the rest of the predicate. This can be done by expansion exercises in which the new elements must be put within the predicate:

Karl hat gearbeitet; ⌐*mit seinem Freund*⌐

Karl hat ⌐*mit seinem Freund*⌐ *gearbeitet*.

Exercises can take the form of successive expansion of the central area of the German sentence:

Karl hat ⌐*mit seinem Freunde*⌐ *gearbeitet*; *immer*

Karl hat ⌐*immer mit seinem Freunde*⌐ *gearbeitet*.

An alternative approach to teaching the difference between these segments of the German sentence is to start with present-tense constructions and convert them into the perfect (or other compound tenses):

Karl arbeitet ⌐*mit seinem Freund*⌐.

Karl hat ⌐*mit seinem Freund*⌐ *gearbeitet*.

4.   How much time should be spent in teaching word order within the central area of the sentence is debatable. The restrictions in word order within this area are actually fairly complicated. Most German sentences that the beginning student will want to form are unlikely to conflict with these restrictions. The following sentences are equally possible:

Karl hat ⌐*seinem Freund das Buch*⌐ *gegeben*.

Karl hat ⌐*das Buch seinem Freund*⌐ *gegeben*.

An adverb like *gern* or *gestern* could be placed before, between, or after the noun phrases. Therefore the sentences above could appear with all possible permutations of *das Buch*, *gestern*, and *seinem Freund* within the central area. The choice of one order as opposed to the other would depend on various circumstances and express rather subtle differences that have, in fact, not been described with great precision or agreement by researchers in German syntax. In general it can be stated that the freedom of choice which the speaker of German enjoys in arranging word order allows him to procede from the "known" to the "unknown"— or perhaps from the "known" to the "goal" of the sentence. Thus in the sentence *Karl hat* ⌐*gestern seinem Freund das Buch*⌐ *gegeben*, the stressed element of the sentence is likely to be *das Buch*. And the "goal" of the communication *Karl hat* ⌐*gestern das Buch seinem Freund*⌐ *gegeben*, presupposes a stress on *Freund*, with the implication that the giving of the book to his friend (and not to someone else) is the important communication of the sentence. Similarly, the arrangement *Karl hat* ⌐*seinem Freund das Buch gestern*⌐ *gegeben* seems to imply that *gestern* is the point to be emphasized in the sentence. However, it is far more important to teach the beginning student the restrictions in freedom of word order than to explain to him the subtle differences in meaning expressed by the possible permutations. Perhaps the main restriction within the central area that should be taught on the elementary level concerns the position of the direct and indirect object pronouns. Within the area the direct object and the indirect object pronoun occupy the initial section: **D.Obj.P./Ind.Obj.P.**

It is possible to say *Karl hat* $\boxed{immer\ seinem\ Freund\ das\ Geld}$ *gegeben;* but with pronoun replacement the sentence must become *Karl hat* $\boxed{es\ ihm\ immer}$ *gegeben.*

At the end of the **central section**, we normally place adverbs of manner and especially adverbial expressions of place. The latter, which are modifications of the verb, can perhaps be considered as part of the verb section:

Robert geht $\boxed{mit\ seinem\ Freund\ nach\ Hause.}$

or

Robert geht $\boxed{mit\ seinem\ Freund}$ *nach Hause.*

The central area may be considered as composed of three possible sections: an initial section that contains the pronouns, a solid core that consists of the noun objects, and a final section that contains adverbs: *Er hat* $\boxed{ihm\ das\ Buch\ sofort}$ *gegeben.*

5. The cases in which the order finite verb + subject rather than subject + finite verb is required should be drilled from the beginning of the course. Actually there are only two basic reasons for the finite verb + subject order:

(a) It is used in a question: *Hat Karl* $\boxed{seinem\ Freund\ das\ Buch}$ *geben wollen?*

(b) It is used whenever any **one** element of the $\boxed{central}$ or final predicate section is put in the initial position: *Karl hat* $\boxed{seinem\ Freund\ das\ Buch\ gestern}$ *geben wollen* can become $\boxed{Seinem\ Freund}$ *hat Karl* $\boxed{das\ Buch\ gestern}$ *geben wollen,* or $\boxed{Gestern}$ *hat Karl* $\boxed{seinem\ Freund\ das\ Buch}$ *geben wollen.*

In connection with (b) above, it should be noted that the object pronoun—especially if it is unstressed—is often not separated from the finite verb and may become interpolated between the finite verb and the succeeding subject: *Karl gibt* $\boxed{ihm\ das\ Buch}$. $\neq$ *Hat* $\boxed{ihm}$ *Karl* $\boxed{das\ Buch}$ *gegeben?*

Since we can think of subordinate clauses as replacements of other parts of speech, the rule that a preceding subordinate clause also brings about the finite verb + subject order is implied in what has been stated. Replacing the adverb *gestern* of the sentence *Gestern hat Karl . . .* by an adverbial clause, we obtain, *Weil er Angst hatte, hat Karl . . .*

The possibility of moving elements from the central or predicate section is subject to certain restrictions. Some of these restrictions affect pronouns: *Robert hat* *ihn (den Mann) gern* *gesehen* can become *Ihn* *hat Robert* *gern* *gesehen*; but *Robert hat* *es (das Buch) gern* *gesehen* cannot be transformed to **Es* *hat Robert* *gern* *gesehen* because *es* can be accusative as well as nominative, and the last sentence would normally be interpreted as *Es hat* *Robert gern* *gesehen*, with *es* being a replacement for *das Mädchen* or *das Kind*.

Putting elements other than the subject into the initial position is a device used fairly frequently in spoken German. However, without considerable practice, the student may neither use nor understand the device. Exercises practicing the construction can consist of the student putting successive elements of a sentence into initial position:

Ich habe *mit meinem Freund gestern* *nicht gesprochen.*
1. *Mit meinem Freund* *habe ich* *gestern* *nicht gesprochen.*
2. *Gestern* *habe ich* *mit meinem Freund* *nicht gesprochen.*
3. *Gesprochen habe ich* *mit meinem Freund gestern* *nicht.*

Even the beginning student should be able to understand the procedure of putting an element into the initial position. The meaning of initial position can be best approached from the already mentioned idea that German syntax allows—within its rigid framework—a progression from the known to the unknown. The initial position is typically utilized to refer to the preceding statement, to tie the sentence in with a previous observation or question. While the end of the sentence generally contains a stressed element that is the goal of the communication, the initial position refers to its starting point. Thus sentence 1, above, is likely to be used in response to a question such as *Ja, was sagt denn Ihr Freund dazu?* It ties the sentence to the question in which the *Freund* is mentioned. Sentence 2 is likely to be the response to a statement or question containing a time reference: *Haben Sie Ihren Freund gestern gesehen? Was haben Sie gestern gemacht? Was hat Ihr Freund gestern gesagt?* Sentence 3 is only conceivable as response to a statement or question using the word *gesprochen*, for example, *Haben Sie mit Ihrem Freund gesprochen?*, *Wann haben Sie mit Ihrem Freund gesprochen?* It takes the word *gesprochen* as its starting point and proceeds to its goal with the word *nicht*, denying specifically the word *gesprochen* and thus inviting a follow-up, such as *aber ich habe ihn gesehen:* *I did not* | *speak* | *to my friend, but I* | *saw* | *him.*

In the more or less normal order in which the subject precedes the verb, the subject standing in front position is of course the known element from which the sentence procedes and about which it gives new information. However, there are instances in which even the subject of the sentence is unknown and not tied in with previous statements. It is interesting to note that in such cases German syntax does indeed not put the subject in the initial position, but in a stressed "goal" position toward the end of the sentence: *Es lebte einmal ein mächtiger König . . . Es war einmal ein Mann . . . Es reiten drei Reiter zum Tore hinaus.* Statements such as these (the first two typically found at the beginning of fairy tales) will occur in a situation in which the statement and its subject cannot be tied to any previous communication. The statements just quoted are examples of sentences that have no known starting point from which to procede. Since there is no starting point, the sentence should begin with the verb. However, initial position of the verb is reserved for the question. Sentences without starting point or tie-in to a previous sentence are therefore preceded by the word *es*. This pronoun is best explained as a **nonquestion marker**. It certainly is not the grammatical subject. As a matter of fact, we must be careful to distinguish this nonquestion marker *es* from the *es* which is the grammatical subject of impersonal verbs (for instance, *es regnet*) and which—unlike the nonquestion marker—can appear in positions other than the sentence-initial (such as *Regnet es heute?*).

The possibility of the finite verb moving to the end of the sentence is restricted to the subordinate clause that starts with a conjunction, a relative clause, or an indirect question. This particular position of the finite verb is obviously best practiced in connection with exercises in which main clauses are changed into subordinate ones:

Karl hat | *immer mit seinem Freund* | *gearbeitet.*
Ich weiss, dass Karl | *immer mit seinem Freund* | *gearbeitet hat.*

or

Karl konnte | *unsere Antwort* | *nicht verstehen.*
Ich weiss, dass Karl | *unsere Antwort* | *nicht verstehen konnte.*

The final position in the sentence of the finite verb accounts also for the possibility of the finite form of a so-called separable-prefix verb appearing in combination with the prefix. Normally the prefix and the stem of a verb, such as *antreten, eintreffen, ankommen,* would appear together only in the infinitive form: *Der Zug wird um sechs Uhr ankommen.*

The past participle shows the separation of the prefix from the stem: *Der Zug ist um sechs Uhr angekommen*. If the simple finite verb is used in the main clause, the stem appears as finite verb and the separable prefix belongs to the final predicate section: *Der Zug kommt* ⎡*heute um sechs Uhr*⎤ *an*; but the transformation into the subordinate clause will combine the separable prefix and the finite form: *Ich weiss, dass der Zug* ⎡*um sechs Uhr*⎤ *ankommt*.

(B) THE REPLACEMENT OPERATIONS

No matter what particular method of instruction we may use, we can assume that the student will, or might, create most of his own sentences by somehow operating on models which he has learned. The rest of our discussion of German syntax will therefore be devoted to a quick analysis of precisely those operations involved in the creation of sentences. The basic operation—and the most simple—is the one of substitution. The student creates a new sentence without changing the syntactical model. As we have emphasized already, the problem of creating new sentences by substitution procedures alone is primarily a morphological one which we have dealt with in our discussion of morphology. Purely syntactical problems in the substitution process are comparatively rare but may arise for several reasons: the substitution process may bring about a change in the syntactical pattern, or the student may substitute wrongly because he is not aware of the word class of the substitution word which he is using. To give an example of the first category: normally the substitution of pronoun for noun does not change the syntactical pattern: *Ich sehe* ⎡*den Mann*⎤ ≠ *Ich sehe* ⎡*ihn*⎤ : *Ich gebe* ⎡*Karl das Buch*⎤ ≠ *Ich gebe* ⎡*ihm das Buch*⎤. However, if we substitute pronouns for both objects of the last sentence, we obtain the word order *Ich gebe* ⎡*es ihm*⎤ (never *ihm es), since with pronouns the direct object must always precede the indirect one. The previously mentioned necessity of putting the object pronouns at the beginning of the central area of the sentence furnishes another example of a syntactical change brought about by substitution: *Ich habe* ⎡*gestern abend meinem Freund ein Buch*⎤ *gegeben*. The pronoun replacement furnishes *Ich habe* ⎡*es ihm gestern abend*⎤ *gegeben*, not *gestern abend es ihm. This usage seems best explained by the fact that the pronoun objects are usually unstressed and cannot be separated from the preceding finite verb.

A fairly typical syntactical error caused by the misunderstanding of a word category is the replacement of an adverb by a conjunction. A coordinating conjunction (such as *aber, sondern, oder, denn*) is not an integral member of a sentence; it merely links the sentence to another. Thus the sentence that starts with the coordinating conjunction follows the word order <u>subject</u> + <u>finite verb</u>. This is quite different from the situation in which an adverb is moved into the first position and for which the order <u>finite verb</u> + <u>subject</u> is required: *Aber <u>mein Freund</u> hat recht*, but *Trotzdem* (adverb) *hat <u>mein Freund recht</u>*. There is further the possibility that the student may mistake a coordinating conjunction for a subordinating one, which introduces a subordinate clause and relegates the <u>finite verb</u> into final position: *Obgleich <u>mein Freund recht hat</u>; Trotzdem hat <u>mein Freund</u> recht; Aber <u>mein Freund</u> hat recht.*

Failure to assign the conjunction or adverb involved into the correct word category will result in faulty word order. Thus exercises contrasting adverbs and the two types of conjunctions may be necessary to make the student aware of the fundamental difference between these word classes:

TEACHER: *Wir werden siegen. Wir haben recht. . . . weil_____ .*

STUDENT: *Wir werden siegen, weil wir recht haben.*

TEACHER: _____ . *. . . denn_____ .*

STUDENT: *Wir werden siegen, denn wir haben recht.*

TEACHER: _____ . *. . . deshalb_____ .*

STUDENT: *Wir werden siegen; deshalb haben wir recht.*

(C) TRANSFORMATION OPERATIONS

The negative transformation of English is basically accomplished by the negative **not** being applied to an auxiliary verb (*have, be, may, can,* and so on): *I have seen him ≠ I have not seen him; I can see him ≠ I cannot see him.* If the sentence to be made negative does not contain an auxiliary verb, then a "dummy" auxiliary (namely, *do*) must be put into the negative sentence: *I speak English ≠ I do not speak English.* In German the situation is very different and in a sense much simpler. If the verb is to be negated, then the basic position of the negative adverb *nicht* is at the beginning of the verb section after the central section of the sentence:

<u>Ich lese</u> das Buch .   *<u>Ich lese</u> das Buch <u>nicht</u>.*

<u>Ich habe</u> das Buch <u>gelesen</u>.   *<u>Ich habe</u> das Buch <u>nicht gelesen</u>.*

<u>Ich kann</u> das Buch <u>lesen</u>.   *<u>Ich kann</u> das Buch <u>nicht lesen</u>.*

Ich *habe* ⌐*das Buch*⌐ *lesen müssen*   *Ich* *habe* ⌐*das Buch*⌐ *nicht lesen*
                                              müssen.

Ich *bin* ⌐*mit ihm*⌐ *dorthin gefahren.*   *Ich* *bin* ⌐*mit ihm*⌐ *nicht dorthin*
                                              gefahren.

Gesprochen *habe* *ich* ⌐*mit dem*   *Gesprochen* *habe* *ich* ⌐*mit dem*
   Jungen⌐.   *Jungen*⌐ *nicht.*

There is also the possibility of *nicht* as verbal negation appearing in the initial finite-verb area.

Ich *spreche* ⌐*mit dem Jungen*⌐.   *Ich* *spreche nicht* ⌐*mit dem*
                                              Jungen⌐.

However, this possibility is utilized less frequently and is subject to certain restrictions. Thus *nicht* could not be used as verb negation after the finite verb and before the succeeding pronoun: in *Ich gebe ihm das Buch* the verb could not be negated by saying *Ich gebe nicht ihm das Buch.* The unstressed pronoun following the finite verb cannot be separated from it by the negation.

The negation *nicht* can, however, be used quite freely in almost any position for the purpose of specifically negating the clause element before which it appears. In such cases the succeeding clause element is usually heavily stressed. Thus the last sentence quoted in the paragraph above is possible if *ihm* receives a heavy stress: *Ich gebe nicht* ⌐*ihm*⌐ *das Buch* (*sondern seinem Bruder*). This usage is comparable to the usage of *not* in English for the purpose of negating a specific element of the sentence other than the verb: *I give the book not to him* (*but to his brother*).

The best way of practicing the position of *nicht* as a negation of the verb is in a series of exercises in which the student makes positive statements negative:

Ich gebe meinem Freund das Buch.   *Ich gebe meinem Freund das Buch*
                                              nicht.

Especially important are exercises in which the student practices putting *nicht* into the predicate area in a position preceding other elements of that portion of the sentence:

Ich *gebe* ⌐*auf meinen Freund*⌐ *acht.*   *Ich* *gebe* ⌐*auf meinen Freund*⌐
                                              nicht acht.

Ich *reise* ⌐*heute morgen*⌐ *ab.*   *Ich* *reise* ⌐*heute morgen*⌐ *nicht ab.*
Ich *habe* ⌐*mit Karl heute*⌐   *Ich* *habe* ⌐*mit Karl heute*⌐ *nicht*
   gesprochen.   *gesprochen.*

Ich habe │das Buch gestern│   Ich habe │das Buch gestern│ nicht
gelesen.   gelesen.

In connection with the type of exercise above, we must point to the necessity of the student's recognizing verbal expressions or verbal complements that form part of the predicate section and are preceded by the negation. Basically, verbal complements such as *in Bezug* (*nehmen*), *in Bewegung* (*setzen*), *in Angriff* (*nehmen*) follow the same syntactical patterns as the separable prefixes of the verb and should therefore be learned as part of the verb: *angreifen, abnehmen, niedersetzen;* and in the same way: *in Bewegung setzen, in Angriff nehmen,* and so on:

Ich setze │den Krug│ nieder.   Ich setze │den Krug│ nicht nieder.
Ich setze │den Motor│ in Bewegung.   Ich setze │den Motor│ nicht in
                                                            Bewegung.

The negative transformation produced through the use of the negative adjective *keine* does not offer any particular problems. Some students may use the German *nicht*-transformation instead of *keine*, and produce sentences that, depending on the context, may sound either wrong or stilted, such as **Ich habe Freunde **nicht*** instead of *Ich habe keine Freunde.* As a general rule we can state that German uses *keine* in equivalence to English (*not*) *any.* This equation opens up the danger of some students trying to introduce a double negation following the English pattern of *I have not any friends.* The result is genuine substandard double negative in German (*keine . . . nicht*). Equating *kein* with the English *no* (*I have no children*) eliminates this danger but may make the correct use of *kein* dependent on a specific English cue. The student may have to be told specifically not to use any second negation with *keine* and go through pattern drills of this type:

> *Haben Sie Kinder?*   *Nein, ich habe keine Kinder.*
> *Haben Sie Geld?*   *Nein, ich habe kein Geld.*

Another error that may occur in connection with negation is the equating of *nicht* with other negative adverbs: *nie, niemals, nimmer.* In fact, the syntactical privileges of *nicht*, on the one hand, and *nie, niemals*, etc., on the other, do not completely overlap. As far as position within the sentence goes, they do agree, but *nie, nimmer, niemals* can be used as adverbs in sentence-stress (initial) position: *Nie sollst du mich befragen. Nicht* may not be used in this position, except in dramatic or poetic language.

The interrogative transformation of English is accomplished by putting the auxiliary verb at the beginning of the sentence: *I may go home ≠ May I go home? They have left ≠ Have they left?* If the sentence to be put in the interrogative does not contain an auxiliary, then the form of *do* must be used: *He speaks English ≠ Does he speak English?* If an interrogative pronoun or adverb is used, it precedes the auxiliary: *He speaks English ≠ When does he speak English?* If the interrogative pronoun is the subject of the sentence, no interrogative transformation is necessary: *He knows the answer ≠ Who knows the answer?*

The mechanism behind the interrogative transformation of German is basically quite different. It consists simply of putting the verb into the initial position whenever there is no interrogative pronoun or adverb and of putting the latter into the initial position whenever they are used. The reversal of the order <u>subject</u> + <u>verb</u> to <u>verb</u> + <u>subject</u> is, in a sense, the automatic result of those operations: *Er spricht* $\boxed{deutsch}$ *≠ Spricht er* $\boxed{deutsch}$*?* $\boxed{Warum}$ *spricht er* $\boxed{deutsch}$*?* (just as $\boxed{Heute}$ *spricht er* $\boxed{deutsch}$).

Even though the basic mechanism of the interrogative transformation is different in each language, they do produce an overlap in certain cases, at least as far as the order of subject and verb is concerned. German, as English, does not use any interrogative transformation if the interrogative pronoun happens to be the subject: *Wer weiss die Antwort? Who knows the answer?* Both languages agree in simply reversing the order of <u>subject</u> + <u>finite verb</u> if the verb is an auxiliary: *Er kann sprechen; Kann er sprechen? He can speak; Can he speak?*

The student should thus have comparatively little trouble with the interrogative transformation of German. In the cases in which the languages do not agree, namely, the application of the transformation to constructions not involving auxiliaries, there is usually little temptation to transfer the more complicated English procedure involving the auxiliary *do* to German. Troubles are more likely to develop if the interrogative transformation is applied to the negative sentence. In this case English will normally not separate the negation from the auxiliary: *He doesn't speak with his friend ≠ Doesn't he speak with his friend?* In German the negation could never be interpolated between <u>finite verb</u> and <u>subject</u>; *Er spricht nicht mit seinen Freund ≠ Spricht er nicht mit seinem Freund?* but never **Spricht nicht er . . .* which is a construction an American may produce under the influence of *Doesn't he speak . . .?*

The passive transformation of German follows this simple rule: the finite form of the verb or the infinitive is replaced by the corresponding form of *werden* and is simultaneously transformed into the past participle:

Ich glaube zu lieben	*Ich glaube geliebt zu werden*
Ich liebe	*Ich werde geliebt*
Ich liebte	*Ich wurde geliebt*

As shall be pointed out later, the passive of the compound tenses is better explained as the past or future modification of the passive of other tenses:

Ich werde geschlagen	*Ich werde geschlagen werden*
Ich werde geschlagen	*Ich bin geschlagen worden*

The German passive transformation offers several problems to the speaker of English. One of the most important is that the English counterpart of the German passive is formed by *be* + participle. Therefore the student will have a tendency to form his German passive by *sein* + participle: *Er ist geschlagen* instead of *Er wird geschlagen*. *Sein* + past participle is, of course, a possible construction in German that does not express action, but a state. The very concept of state versus action is not clearly expressed in English and may cause problems. *The door was closed* can be *Die Tür war geschlossen* as well as *Die Tür wurde geschlossen*. Adding the agent will normally help to clarify the situation: *The door was closed by his friend/Die Tür wurde von seinem Freund geschlossen; Then the door was closed/Dann war die Tür geschlossen*. Another problem connected with the passive is created by the English habit of making an indirect object into a nominative subject of a passive sentence: *He gave me some money/I was given some money*. The corresponding German transformation is *Er gab mir Geld/Mir* (not *ich*) *wurde Geld gegeben*. In other words, German retains the dative in the passive transformation. In order to impress this feature of German on the student, he should be asked to perform passive transformations on sentences such as the following:

Karl hat mir Geld gegeben.	*Mir wurde von Karl Geld gegeben.*
Karl hat mir eine Geschichte erzählt.	*Mir wurde von Karl eine Geschichte erzählt.*

One of the important functions of the passive in German is to describe the action as such—without having to refer to the actor. As a matter of fact, German has two ways of expressing action without naming the actor: the passive and the pronoun *man*: *Im Kino lacht man sehr viel* or *Im Kino wird viel gelacht*. English has really no such handy ways of describing action as such. If there is an object, or something like an object, involved, English can use a passive: *English is spoken in many parts of the world*. But in most cases English will express "action without actor" by using the pronouns *they* or *you* (without referring to anybody in particular): *In many parts of the world they speak English*, or *In the United States you pay a lot of taxes*. The student must be made aware of the fact that the normal German equivalent is an impersonal passive or a construction using *man* as subject. This can be done in translation exercises contrasting the English and German usage:

They danced a lot.   *Es wurde sehr viel getanzt.*
         Man tanzte sehr viel.

The *es* of the sentence *Es wurde sehr viel getanzt* is not the subject of the sentence. Since the passive construction is here used to denote action as such, there is no subject. But since there is none, the finite verb appears in the first position. This necessitates the use of the nonquestion marker *es*. The best proof that *es* is simply the nonquestion marker and not the subject comes from the fact that it immediately vanishes if another sentence element is moved into the initial position. In order to impress this automatic vanishing of *es* upon the student, exercises such as the following may be necessary:

Es wird viel getanzt.
Heute: *Heute wird viel getanzt.*

(D) EXPANSION OPERATIONS

1. Verb Expansion

One of the most important ways of creating new sentences is to take an existing sentence and enlarge it by adding to the noun or verb phrases. Turning our attention first to ways of expanding the **verb** part of the sentence, we want to point out that the past modification can be thought of as precisely such a way of expanding the verb phrase.

The Past Modification

The past modification of German corresponds in form quite closely to that used in English. The English construction is brought about by replacing any simple form of the verb by the corresponding form of **have** + **past participle**:

he ***comes***   *he* ***has come***
he will ***come***   *he will* ***have come***

*he could **come***	*he could **have come***
*he **came***	*he **had come***
***coming** home*	***having come** home* . . .

The German past modification works basically the same way: The principal way in which it is brought about is by replacing any simple form of the verb by the corresponding form of **haben** + **past participle**:

*ich **spreche***	*ich **habe gesprochen***
*ich **sprach***	*ich **hatte gesprochen***
*ich hoffe **zu sprechen***	*ich hoffe* . . . ***gesprochen zu haben***

There are, however, several problems connected with the German past modification.

1. With many words, German uses the auxiliary *sein* (rather than *haben*) for its past modification (or expansion):

ich weiss   *ich habe gewusst*

but

ich gehe   *ich bin gegangen*

There are various ways of classifying the verbs that take the *sein*-conjugation: verbs of motion (such as *gehen, fahren, laufen, kommen*) and verbs signifying a change or development (such as *passieren, geschehen, vorfallen, sterben, wachsen, verhungern, erbleichen, erkranken*). The semantic labels do not define the categories too clearly. Therefore the student must ultimately learn the specific verbs that are conjugated with *sein*. All the verbs that take *sein* are intransitive, that is, they do not take an accusative object. (There are a few words that use *sein* if they are used intransitively, but switch to *haben* if they are used with an accusative: *Ich bin nach Berlin gefahren*, but *Ich habe den Wagen gefahren*.) However, since not all intransitive verbs are necessarily conjugated with *sein*, the teacher must be careful not to establish an association of intransitive verb + *sein* in the student's mind.

Haben is conjugated with *haben*: *Er hat Geld/Er hat Geld gehabt*. *Sein* and *werden* are conjugated with *sein*: *Er ist in Berlin/Er ist in Berlin gewesen; Er wird krank/Er ist krank geworden*. If the past modification is applied to *werden*, used in the passive transformation, the past participle form *worden* (not *geworden*) is used: *Er wird geschlagen/Er ist geschlagen worden*. It may be necessary to contrast the past modification of sentences such as *Er wird krank* and *Er wird geschlagen* in special exercises.

2. The rule that any simple form of the verb is subject to the past transformation has certain restrictions. *Werden* (in the meaning of future modification) and *sein* or *haben* (in the meaning of past transformation) are not subject to further past transformation: the *wird* of *Er wird gehen*, the *ist* of *Er ist gegangen*, and the *hat* of *Er hat gelacht* cannot be transformed into *ist geworden*, *ist gewesen*, and *hat gehabt*. Of course, the *wird* (passive) of *Er wird geschlagen* is subject to the past modification: *Er ist geschlagen worden;* so are the *ist* of *Er ist krank/Er ist krank gewesen* and *hat* of *Er hat Geld/Er hat Geld gehabt*.

3. One of the outstanding differences between English and German is the fact that German allows the past modification of its modal auxiliaries. Thus in the German sentence *Er muss arbeiten*, the modal auxiliary is subject to the past transformation: *Er hat arbeiten müssen*. As we shall point out in the discussion of modification by modals, this sentence must be differentiated from *Er muss gearbeitet haben* (which is the result of the modification by *müssen* of *Er hat gearbeitet*).

4. Another problem connected with the past transformation is created by the English ≠ German difference in the use of *haben* ≠ *have*. English uses *have* as an auxiliary to denote past modification and as a genuine verb to indicate possession. These uses parallel those of German *haben*. In addition, English uses *have to* quite frequently to denote obligation with about the same meaning as *must* (German *müssen*). The use of *haben* to denote obligation is comparatively rare and restricted to denote compulsion from without rather than internal obligation, for instance, *Was habe ich denn hier zu tun?* = *What have I to* (*am I to, should I*) *do here?* Furthermore, English uses *have* also to denote causation: *I have the windows washed every six months*. This sentence literally translated into German could result in a meaningful sentence: *Jede sechs Monate have ich die Fenster geputzt*. The meaning of the German sentence is of course, totally different from that of the English counterpart. Therefore the student must be expressly warned that German *haben* never carries the meaning of causation. He must become familiar with the use of German *lassen*, a use which incidentally also involves a minor problem: if the infinitive succeeding *lassen* describes an action that can be performed by the dependent object, *lassen* indicates permission; if the succeeding infinitive describes an action performed on the object, it indicates causation. Thus we have *Ich habe die Bilder malen lassen* (causation), but *Ich habe den Mann gehen lassen* (permission). For the beginning student, at least, the main problem of the German past modification is probably the purely technical one of preserving the right word order, that is,

putting the auxiliary into the <u>verb</u> position and throwing the past participle into the <u>predicate field</u>. Many exercises involving the past transformation are necessary to make this German speech habit automatic:

<u>Ich</u> <u>spreche</u> | mit meinem Freund | .   <u>Ich</u> <u>habe</u> | mit meinem Freund | <u>gesprochen</u>.
<u>Ich</u> <u>gebe</u> | meinem Freund das Buch | .   <u>Ich</u> <u>habe</u> | meinem Freund das Buch | <u>gegeben</u>.

There are several additional problems connected with this placement of the past participle in the <u>predicate field</u>. In the past modification of the modal auxiliaries and of the <u>verbs</u> *sehen* and *lassen*, the infinitive form (rather than the past participle) appears after another infinitive in the <u>predicate field</u>:

<u>Ich</u> <u>kann</u> | das Buch | <u>schreiben</u>.   <u>Ich</u> <u>habe</u> | das Buch | <u>schreiben</u> <u>können</u>.
<u>Ich</u> <u>lasse</u> | das Buch | <u>schreiben</u>.   <u>Ich</u> <u>habe</u> | das Buch | <u>schreiben</u> <u>lassen</u>.
<u>Ich</u> <u>sehe</u> | den Jungen | <u>arbeiten</u>.   <u>Ich</u> <u>habe</u> | den Jungen | <u>arbeiten</u> <u>sehen</u>.

The past transformation brings out the difference between separable and nonseparable verbs. With separable verbs the preposition or adverb that makes up the first element stands already in the predicate field, even in the simple tense: <u>Ich</u> <u>höre</u> | mir die Oper | <u>an</u>. In the past modification, the past participle is separated from the preposition or adverb by the *ge*-prefix: <u>Ich</u> <u>habe</u> | mir die Oper | <u>angehört</u>. With nonseparable verbs the initial syllable (*be-, ent-, emp, ge-, miss-, ver-, zer-*) stands before the verb in the simple tense and remains there in all the compound tenses.

<u>Ich</u> <u>empfange</u> | die Botschaft | .   <u>Ich</u> <u>habe</u> | die Botschaft | <u>empfangen</u>.

As we have stressed before, the confusion between the treatment of separable and nonseparable verbs can be avoided by a great deal of practice and by remembering the verbs involved with their correct pronunciation: **all separable verbs have the primary word stress on the first syllable**.

A problem of confusion between separable and nonseparable treatment of verbs is created by a limited number of verbs beginning with *durch-, um-, über-, unter-*, or *wieder-*. Since some of these verbs can be either separable or unseparable, the problem consists simply of the student's remembering the meaning of the separable usage as opposed to the unseparable one,

OUTLINE CHART OF GERMAN TENSES

All the tenses of German are derived from the four basic tenses (present and simple past, indicative and subjunctive) according to the following pattern of successive transformations and modifications:

[four basic tenses]

Pres. Indic. (A)	Subj. I (B)
er ruft	*er rufe*
Simple Past Indic. (C)	Subj. II (D)
er rief	*er riefe*

PASSIVE TRANSFORMATION (P)

Pres. Indic. Pass. (A+P)	Subj. I Pass. (B+P)
er wird gerufen	*er werde gerufen*
Past Indic. Pass. (C+P)	Subj. II Pass. (D+P)
er wurde gerufen	*er würde gerufen*

PAST MODIFICATION (Pt)

Compound Past (Perf.) (A+Pt)	Past Subj. I (B+Pt)	Compound Past Pass. Indic. (A+P+Pt)	Past Subj. I Pass. (B+P+Pt)
er hat gerufen	*er habe gerufen*	*er ist gerufen worden*	*er sei gerufen worden*
Pluperf. (C+Pt)	Past Subj. II (D+Pt)	Pluperf. Pass. Indic. (C+P+Pt)	Past Subj. II Pass. (D+P+Pt)
er hatte gerufen	*er hätte gerufen*	*er war gerufen worden*	*er wäre gerufen worden*

FUTURE (MODAL) MODIFICATION (F)

Fut. (A+F)	Fut. Subj. I (B+F)	Fut. Pass. (A+P+F)	Fut. Pass. Subj. I (B+P+F)
er wird rufen	*er werde rufen*	*er wird gerufen werden*	*er werde gerufen werden*
	Fut. Subj. II (D+F)		Fut. Pass. Subj. II (D+P+F)
	er würde rufen		*er würde gerufen werden*
Fut. Perf. (A+Pt+F)	Fut. Perf. Subj. I (B+Pt+F)	Fut. Perf. Pass. (A+P+Pt+F)	Fut. Perf. Pass. Subj. I (B+P+Pt+F)
er wird gerufen haben	*er werde gerufen haben*	*er wird gerufen worden sein*	*er werde gerufen worden sein*
	Fut. Perf. Subj. II (D+Pt+F)		Fut. Perf. Pass. Subj. II (D+P+Pt+F)
	er würde gerufen haben		*er würde gerufen worden sein*

for example, *Ich wiederhole die Aufgabe* (repeat)/*Ich habe die Aufgabe wiederholt*, but *Ich hole das Buch wieder* (get back)/*Ich habe das Buch wiedergeholt*. Just remembering *'wiederholen* vs. *wieder'holen* does not do much good, unless we also remember which means which. Usually the literal meaning calls for the separable prefix, whereas the figurative meaning requires the nonseparable use.

Modal Modification

The uses of modals in German and English resemble each other in many important ways. In both languages the modal expansion is to be distinguished from the construction of verb + infinitive (connected by *zu*, or *to*). *Ich schreibe/Ich kann schreiben*, *I write/I can write;* but *Ich fange an zu schreiben*, *I begin to write*. In both languages, there are a few verbs which imitate the modal expansion by being followed by the infinitive without the connecting *zu*, or *to*: *Ich höre ihn singen*, *I hear him sing; Ich lasse ihn schreiben*, *I let him write*. In both languages the modal expansion operates in basically the same way. Any simple form of the verb (present, imperfect) can be replaced by the corresponding form of the modal while the verb is transformed into the infinitive form:

English:	*I write*	⟶ *I can write*
	he writes	⟶ *he can write*
	he wrote	⟶ *he could write*
German:	*ich schreibe*	⟶ *ich kann schreiben*
	er schreibt	⟶ *er kann schreiben*
	er schrieb	⟶ *er konnte schreiben*

There are, however, important differences between German and English. We have already mentioned that German—unlike English—can apply the past modification to the modal auxiliaries:

Ich kann arbeiten ⟶ *Ich habe arbeiten können* (*I was able to work*)
Ich muss arbeiten ⟶ *Ich habe arbeiten müssen* (*I had to work*)

In addition, German can apply one modification to another:

Er kann singen ⟶ *Er mag singen können* (*He can probably sing*)

Most important, German can apply the future modification to other modals:

Er kann singen ⟶ *Er wird singen können* (*He will be able to sing*)
Er muss singen ⟶ *Er wird singen müssen* (*He will have to sing*)

Furthermore it is possible in German to apply the modal modification to the infinitive:

Ich glaube, ihn zu verstehen → *Ich glaube, ihn verstehen zu können*
Ich glaube zu arbeiten ⟶ *Ich glaube arbeiten zu müssen*

The future modification—replacement of the present by the corresponding form of *werden* and transformation into the infinitive—is best considered as a special case of the modal modification: the modification of *Er arbeitet* ⟶ *Er wird arbeiten* operates on the same principle as *Er arbeitet* ⟶ *Er muss arbeiten*.

The German future is simply the future modification of the present:

Er schlägt ⟶ *Er wird schlagen*
Er wird geschlagen → *Er wird geschlagen werden*

The future modification of the compound past results in the future perfect:

Ich habe geschlagen → *Ich werde geschlagen haben*

The future modification of the subjunctive results in the future subjunctive I and future subjunctive II (conditional):

Er schlage → *Er werde schlagen*
Er schlüge → *Er würde schlagen*

We may also note here that the beginning student may at times be troubled by a confusion between the passive transformation (*werden* + past participle) and the future modification (*werden* + infinitive):

Er wird schlagen   *Er wird geschlagen*

Special exercises contrasting the two operations may be necessary. The problem of confusion may be especially bothersome with verbs using prefixes in the infinitive, thus blurring the differences between the infinitive and the past participle, for example, *Das Buch wird gebraucht; Er wird das Buch gebrauchen.*

One of the most persistent problems is to have the student understand the correct meaning of the German modals and have him use those modals in the intended meaning. This problem of meaning will be treated here (rather than in the next chapter), since it cannot be dissociated from the formal grammar of the modal expansion. Fairly lengthy and correct explanations of the meaning of the German modals are given in most textbooks. Therefore we shall be content with stressing some of the salient facts that may clarify the student's understanding of German usage. The German modals do have a definite meaning:

sollen	obligation (moral)	*Der Mensch soll arbeiten.*
wollen	intention	*Mein Freund will arbeiten.*
können	ability	*Mein Freund kann lesen.*
		Mein Freund kann schwimmen.
dürfen	permission	*Mein Freund darf schwimmen.*
müssen	necessity	*Mein Freund muss seine Aufgabe machen.*
mögen	possibility	*Die Antwort mag richtig sein.*

Warn against confusion with the English future modification: *he will work!* Make up contrasting exercises:

Er wird arbeiten.   Er will arbeiten.

(Whereas some uses of German *wollen* are approaching the meaning of "future," it is better to reserve their discussion for advanced stages of instruction.)

The student must realize that the difficulties with the German modals are created entirely by irregularities or inconsistencies within English grammar. If English modals are negated, it is not always clear whether the negation applies to the modal or to the verb that has been modified. The German negation always applies clearly and unambiguously to the modal itself.

He may not come is an ambiguous English sentence (which can to some extent be clarified by the intonation): *He **may not** come* (negation applied to *may*) means that possibility or permission of coming has been denied (*Er darf nicht kommen*). That the negation applies to *may* rather than *come* is evident if we consider a conversational interchange like *May I come?—No, you may not. He may **not come*** (negation applied to *come*) has a different meaning: the possibility **exists** that the action of coming may not take place (*Er kommt vielleicht nicht*).

When English *must* is negated, the negation is always clearly applied to the main verb and not to the modal: English *He must work* means that the necessity of working exists (*Er muss arbeiten*). However, English *He must not work* establishes that there **is** a necessity of **not working** (and **not** that there is no necessity of working). Thus English *He must not work* does not at all correspond to the German *Er muss nicht arbeiten*. In the latter the *muss* is negated: *There is no necessity of working* (*He does not have to work*). English *He must **not work*** corresponds rather to the German *Er darf nicht arbeiten*. The permission (*darf*) is being negated.

A further conflict between English and German is created by the absence of a special subjunctive form of the modals in English. Thus English *could* and *would* have clearly two functions. They are a past tense: *Whenever he went out to dinner, he would order steak; Since he had a lot of money, he could (was able to) buy a Cadillac.* However, they are also used to indicate nonreality: *If I had money, I would buy a car; If I had money, I could buy a car.* The English auxiliaries *might* and *should* follow the same pattern. The past of *can (could), may (might), shall (should), will (would)* doubles in the function of "contrary to fact"—"unreality." German has its past subjunctive to express the contrary-to-fact function: *Letztes Jahr konnte ich ein Auto kaufen; Wenn ich Geld hätte, könnte (würde, sollte, möchte, dürfte) ich ein Auto kaufen.* To avoid errors caused by such double correspondences as *could/konnte, could/könnte,* it is advisable to devise exercises contrasting sentences such as *Mein Freund konnte mich verstehen; Wenn er mich verstehen könnte, so könnte er mit mir sprechen.*

A final problem—also caused by restriction or irregularity in the English use of the modals—has been alluded to: the English modals (unlike the German) are not capable of future or past modification: *I *will may, I *have might* are impossible in English. The result is that the pupil may have difficulty forming and appreciating the meaning of such German sentences as *Er musste die Wahrheit sagen; Er hat die Wahrheit sagen müssen* vs. *Er muss die Wahrheit gesagt haben. Er **hat** die Wahrheit sagen **müssen** is the past modification of Er **muss** die Wahrheit sagen.* It establishes that necessity existed in the past. *Er **muss** die Wahrheit gesagt **haben*** is the modal modification of *Er **hat** die Wahrheit gesagt.* It applies the idea of *müssen* to *hat* (the past). It means that at present some sort of necessity for a past action is perceived by the speaker. The following is another example:

*Er **kann** jetzt abreisen.* ⟶ (past modification) *Er **hat** abreisen **können**.*

(*He is able to depart.* ⟶ *He was able to depart.*)

but

*Er **ist** abgereist.* ⟶ (modal modification) *Er **kann** abgereist **sein**.*

(*He has departed.* ⟶ *It is possible that he has departed.*)

As we have shown in the discussion of verbal expansion, the German modifications proceed in an orderly fashion. The modal takes the place of the finite verb that is being modified. The verb moves as infinitive (in case of the passive transformation, as past participle) into the end of the predicate field. Thus a sentence like *Er ⁴kann ¹verstanden ²worden ³sein* can be analyzed as having been "created" in exactly the order indicated by its component parts:

passive transformation:	*er ¹versteht* ⟶ *er ²wird ¹verstanden*
past modification:	*er ²wird ¹verstanden* ⟶ *er ³ist ¹verstanden* ²*worden*
modal modification:	*er ³ist ¹verstanden ²worden* ⟶ *er ⁴kann* ¹*verstanden ²worden ³sein* (*he may have been understood*)

The meaning of the sentence can be analyzed in the way indicated above. The speaker perceives some sort of possibility (⁴*kann*) for past performance (³*sein*) of passive action (²*werden*) of ¹*verstehen*.

Er ³hat die Wahrheit ¹sagen ²müssen has been derived from *Er sagt die Wahrheit*

through the modal transformation:	*Er ¹sagt die Wahrheit* ⟶ *Er ²muss die Wahrheit ¹sagen*
and the past transformation:	*Er ²muss die Wahrheit* ¹*sagen* ⟶ *Er ³hat die Wahrheit ¹sagen* ²*müssen.*

In other words, *Er hat die Wahrheit sagen müssen* states that in the past (³*hat*) there existed the necessity (²*müssen*) of telling the truth (¹*sagen*).

Er ³muss die Wahrheit ¹gesagt ²haben, is created from *er sagt die Wahrheit* by the

past transformation:	*Er ¹sagt die Wahrheit* ⟶ *Er ²hat die Wahrheit ¹gesagt*
and the modal transformation:	*Er ²hat die Wahrheit ¹gesagt* ⟶ *Er ³muss die Wahrheit ¹gesagt ²haben.*

As stated above, it indicates that the speaker perceives some sort of necessity (²*muss*) for there having been a past action (³*haben*) of telling the truth (¹*sagen*).

The analytical approach to the modals, which we have just illustrated, is of value as an explanation and can also be used quite profitably to help the student in the comprehension of sentences that contain several successive modifications. When it comes to the actual production of sentences with one or several successive modal expansions, it may be preferable to treat the modal expansions as one unit, for instance, after explaining the meaning of *Das Buch muss von ihm gekauft worden sein*, we can make the student practice the structure involved by suggesting substitution for *das Buch* (*das Heft: Das Heft muss von ihm gekauft worden sein; die Karte: Die Karte muss von ihm gekauft worden sein*) and then by asking for changes in the verb (*verstehen: Das Buch muss von ihm verstanden worden sein; zerreissen: Das Buch muss von ihm zerrissen worden sein*). As a matter of fact, in the practice of the production process of complicated constructions of this type, it may be necessary to use a large number of simple verb or noun substitutions in order to make the construction part of the student's speech habit and divert his attention from the analysis of the structure as such.

Expansion Through Adverbs

In addition to past and modal expansion, there is also the possibility of enlarging the verb phrase by the addition of adverbs or adverbially used phrases (*gestern, am Abend*). The German and English processes resemble each other in many respects. Some of the problems connected with the German adverbial expansion are morphological or semantic and need not be discussed in this context (German uses the adjective as adverb: *Er spricht langsam;* English: *He speaks slowly*). The main problem that affects the syntax of the German adverb is one of position. English has the already mentioned possibility of putting the adverb between the subject and the finite verb (*He often knows*). In German this separation of subject and verb would be impossible. Furthermore, English follows in its adverbial expansion a general sequence of manner, place, time: *Traffic moved slowly on the highway yesterday*. The German order tends to be rather different. As we mentioned in our discussion of word order, the ordering of German adverbs allows a certain amount of freedom. The general tendency is to use the following sequence:

1(a). Adverb of time   *gestern, heute, immer, oft, täglich*
1(b). Adverbial phrase of time   *am Abend, in der Nacht, während des Tages*
2.   Adverbs of manner   *fleissig, rasch, schnell, gern*
3.   Adverb of place   *dort, oben, unten, hinter, rechts, links.*

Er trug ¹gestern ²während unserer Unterhaltung das Buch ³rasch ⁴nach oben. (Note that *das Buch* could precede the adverbs). The error most offensive to the German ear is putting the adverb of place, indicating motion, in the wrong position: *Gehen Sie rasch dorthin; Er hat das Buch schnell in die Tasche gesteckt. Er ist gestern schnell hierher gekommen.* The reason is evidently that the adverb of place (*hierhin, dahin, hinaus, aufwärts, hinunter, von hier, von dort, von oben,* etc.) is really felt as part of the verb and belongs thus in the predicate field at the end of the sentence. As a matter of fact, the difference between the adverb of place and the first part of a separable verb is sometimes difficult to establish. The more the adverb becomes amalgamated with the verb, the more it becomes impossible to place it anywhere except at the beginning of the predicate area. There is a difference in degree rather than in kind between the first elements of *ankommen, herkommen, hierher kommen, nach oben kommen, in die Schule kommen, in der Schule sprechen.* Yet only with the last example, which does not indicate motion, would it be possible to displace the adverbial elements from its position in the predicate field: *Er spricht in der Schule sehr rasch; Er hat in der Schule sehr rasch gesprochen;* but *Er kommt rasch in die Schule; Er ist rasch in die Schule gefahren.*

The best way of practicing adverbial expansion is to give the student exercises in which adverbs are added (or substituted for each other):

Adverb substitution:

	Er geht immer in die Schule.
gern	*Er geht gern in die Schule.*
täglich	*Er geht täglich in die Schule.*

The exercise in which adverbs are added one after the other is, of course, more complicated.

TEACHER: *Er arbeitet.*

STUDENT: *Er arbeitet.*

TEACHER: —————— *gern.*

STUDENT: *Er arbeitet gern.*

TEACHER: —————— *immer* ——— .

STUDENT: *Er arbeitet immer gern.*

TEACHER: ————————————— *in der Schule.*

STUDENT: *Er arbeitet immer gern in der Schule.*

TEACHER: *Er liest.*

STUDENT: *Er liest.*

TEACHER: _____ *in der Schule.*

STUDENT: *Er liest in der Schule.*

TEACHER: _____ *gern* _____ .

STUDENT: *Er liest gern in der Schule.*

TEACHER: _____ *immer* _____ .

STUDENT: *Er liest immer gern in der Schule.*

2. Noun Expansion

Not much need be said about the expansion of the noun or noun phrase as part of the sentence. The English and German processes parallel each other in many ways. The most obvious expansion of the noun (or noun phrases) is the addition of adjectives: *My friend came, My old friend came, My good old friend came.* Similarly, in German: *Mein Freund kam, Mein alter Freund kam, Mein guter alter Freund kam.* What makes the German process difficult is the necessity of using a correct ending for the adjective—a morphological problem discussed previously.

Another possible way of noun-phrase expansion is to have a prepositional expression follow the noun. English is capable of taking any prepositional phrases which follow the verb *be* in the type of sentence *The boy is from Vienna* and of putting it directly after the noun: *the boy from Vienna.* German can follow the same procedure: *Der Junge ist aus Wien, der Junge aus Wien.* One difference between English and German is the indication of possession: English can use a prepositional phrase (*the leg of the dog*) or an inflectional form (*the dog's leg*) to indicate the possessor. There is, in spoken German, a tendency to use prepositional expressions for the indication of possession, but imitation of this trend by the learner must be approached with care: *das Bein von dem Hund* (instead of *des Hundes Bein*) will be accepted by most Germans, but *das Buch von meinem Vater* (instead of *meines Vaters Buch*) is definitely substandard. German and English also follow similar patterns in using nouns or adjectives to form compounds with following nouns: *milk bottle, Milchflasche; German teacher, Deutschlehrer.* In both languages the noun or adjective preceding the noun being modified carries the primary word stress. In German the noun-noun or adjective-noun compound is in fact spelled as one word. The difference between an adjective-noun compound (*Deutschlehrer*) and a noun modified by an adjective (*deutscher Lehrer, ein deutscher Lehrer*) must also be pointed out.

It is only the former that corresponds to the English construction carrying primary stress on the adjective (*'German teacher*), whereas the noun modified by the adjective corresponds to the same construction, which like its German counterpart has the primary stress on the noun (*the German teacher = der deutsche Lehrer*). In the German **adjective-noun compound**, German uses the uninflected form of the adjective, and the adjective modifying the noun uses inflectional endings. In general, at least, the German compound corresponds to the English form, carrying primary stress on the adjective: *'white bread = Weissbrot; 'red wine = 'Rotwein;* but *white 'bread = weisses 'Brot; red 'wine = roter 'Wein.*

German carries noun compounding much farther than English. Noun-noun compounds of the type *filling station attendant* are of course possible in English; but in general the noun-noun compound of English is restricted to a combination of two, and the possibilities of making new compounds are limited. In German it is perfectly legitimate to make up lengthy compounds of one's own, a privilege used (and abused) by many authors. The student reading technical literature has to be prepared to unravel such compounds as *Gesellschaftstheorieentwicklung*, or *Verkehrsmittel-ausnützungmöglichkeit*—words that he will find in no dictionary and that are often the creation of the specific author. But even in ordinary spoken German, such creations as *Arbeitslosenunterstützungsamtsvorstand* are a definite possibility. The best way of handling the problem is to give the student practice in analyzing such compounds, pointing out that they are combined of successive modifications of the last noun used in the compound. Thus the [5]*Donau*/[4]*dampf*/[3]*schifffahrts*/[2]*gesellschafts*/[1]*kapitän* is indeed a *captain* (1) *of a company* (2) *which has ships* (3), *steam ships to be exact* (4), *for the navigation of the Danube* (5). And the [4]*Arbeitslosen*/-[3]*unterstützung*/[2]*amts*/[1]*vorstand* is the *director* (1) *of an office* (2) *concerned with the relief* (3) *of those who are without work* (4).

Another noun-expansion device that may give some trouble to the American student is the use of the modified past or present participle. English, too, can use participles to modify nouns: *an understanding person, a misunderstood woman*, etc. What is not possible in English is to have the participles further modified by a series of adverbs or nouns: *Eine diese Möglichkeit nicht in Betracht ziehende Theorie, Eine vom Verfasser leider nicht erwähnte Möglichkeit.* This type of construction—fairly unusual in spoken German—is a favorite of some literary and many scientific styles of writing. The average student may never want to use the construction but must learn to recognize it. Perhaps the most obvious signal that indicates this kind of construction is the limiting adjective followed by either another limiting adjective (see above *eine diese*) or by a preposition (*eine vom*). The word order in this type of modifying construction is not unlike the one in a subordinate clause. The verb stands at the end of the construction immediately before the noun being modified. The participle construction can be best explained as derived from a sentence the verb of which has been turned into a participle and put at the end of the construction: *Diese Theorie zieht diese Möglichkeit nicht in Betracht; Eine [solche] Theorie ist ausgeschlossen.* The first sentence is now filled into the second one, replacing a modifier (*solche*): *Eine [diese Möglichkeit nicht in Betract ziehende] Theorie ist ausgeschlossen.* The construction under consideration may thus be explained as a transformation that is used as a substitution in another construction. Basically it belongs to the type of structure to be discussed in the next section of this chapter.

(E) REPLACEMENT—TRANSFORMATIONS

The various types of subordinate clauses can best be described and taught as transformations and replacements. They are transformations of a main clause that are then used to replace an element of another main clause. According to the element that is being replaced, we can divide the subordinate clauses into **noun clauses**, **adjectival clauses**, and **adverbial clauses**.

1. Noun Clauses

We can think of a noun clause as a main clause that has been transformed into a subordinate clause and then used to replace a noun or noun phrase (or a pronoun):

(a) *Ich weiss [die Wahrheit].*
(b) *Karl hat gearbeitet.*
Transformation: *. . . dass Karl gearbeitet hat*
Replacement: *Ich weiss, [dass Karl gearbeitet hat].*

Other possibilities of noun clauses are illustrated by the following:

(a) *Ich möchte [die Wahrheit] wissen.*
(b) *Hat Karl die Frage beantwortet?*
Transformation: *. . . ob Karl die Frage beantwortet hat*
Replacement: *Ich möchte wissen, [ob Karl die Frage beantwortet hat].*
(a) *Ich weiss [die Antwort].*
(b) *Wer hat die Frage beantwortet?*
Transformation: *. . . wer die Frage beantwortet hat*
Replacement: *Ich weiss, [wer die Frage beantwortet hat].*

It is, of course, also possible to replace a noun subject by a subordinate clause, for example:

(a) [*Diese Antwort*] *ist sehr unwahrscheinlich.*
(b) *Er hat Recht.*
  [*Dass er Recht hat*] *ist sehr unwahrscheinlich.*

We can note that in the example above, the subordinate clause can be put after the main clause. However, in that case the pronoun *es* must be used as a sort of "dummy" subject. The *es* can be explained as anticipating the real subject (namely the subordinate clause) or again as a marker that keeps the finite verb from occupying the initial position—a word order reserved for the direct question. At any rate, the construction corresponds to English and is not likely to cause much trouble: *It is improbable that he is right/Es ist unwahrscheinlich, dass er Recht hat.*

The main problem connected with the noun-clause operation is likely to be the one that bothers the student with subordinate clauses: the "*Endstellung*" of the finite verb. This problem is best taken care of by practice in converting main clauses into subordinate ones:

1. *Er ist gestern angekommen.*
2. *Er hat mit Karl gesprochen.*
3. *Er spricht französisch.*

Precede the above statements by *ich weiss:*

1. *Ich weiss, dass er gestern angekommen ist.*
2. *Ich weiss, dass er mit Karl gesprochen hat.*
3. *Ich weiss, dass er französisch spricht.*

A noun clause can often represent indirect discourse: *Karl sagt: Ich bin gestern nicht in die Stadt gefahren.* ≠ *Karl sagt, dass er gestern nicht in die Stadt gefahren ist* (*sei, wäre*). *Karl sagt, er ist* (*sei, wäre*) *gestern nicht in die Stadt gefahren.* In connection with this transformation from direct to indirect speech, it should be pointed out to the student that most Germans use the indicative in indirect speech, at least on the colloquial level, although standard literary German requires the subjunctive.

The choice of subjunctive involved is a problem of meaning that we shall refer to again in the last chapter. As we pointed out earlier, and as should be stressed to the student, the choice of the so-called present versus the so-called past forms of the subjunctive have nothing to do with tense. We must also stress that the "*Endstellung*" of the finite verb occurs only if the indirect discourse is introduced by the conjunction *dass*. If there is no conjunction, the finite verb remains in second position in the sentence.

2. Adjectival Clauses

Adjectival clauses can be thought of as main clauses that have been transformed into subordinate clauses and fitted into another sentence in order to replace a descriptive adjective modifying a noun; or they can be considered as the expansion of noun or noun phrase:

(a) *Mein (guter) Freund weiss die Antwort nicht.*
(b) *Mein Freund hat nicht studiert.*
Transformation: *. . . der nicht studiert hat*
Replacement (expansion): *Mein Freund, [der nicht studiert hat,] weiss die Antwort nicht.*

(a) *Mein (guter) Freund weiss die Antwort nicht.*
(b) *Das Buch meines Freundes ist verloren gegangen.*
Transformation: *. . . dessen Buch verloren gegangen ist*
Replacement (expansion): *Mein Freund, [dessen Buch verloren gegangen ist,] weiss die Antwort nicht.*

(a) *Mein (guter) Freund weiss die Antwort nicht.*
(b) *Du hast meinem Freund das Buch nicht gebracht.*
Transformation: *. . . dem du das Buch nicht gebracht hast*
Replacement (expansion): *Mein Freund, [dem du das Buch nicht gebracht hast,] weiss die Antwort nicht.*

(a) *Mein (guter) Freund weiss die Antwort nicht.*
(b) *Du kennst meinen Freund sehr gut.*
Transformation: *. . . den (welchen) du sehr gut kennst*
Replacement (expansion): *Mein Freund, [den du sehr gut kennst], weiss die Antwort nicht.*

Aside from the word-order problem, the adjective clause may give the student the following difficulties: he may mistakenly omit the relative pronoun by following the English construction (*The man I know is your friend*). The student may also be tempted to use *wer* as a relative pronoun on the basis of the equation *wer/who*, which he learns through the interrogative sentence: *Who is that/Wer ist das?* and thus he may say *the man who/*der Mann wer* (instead of *der* or *welcher*).

The last-mentioned problem is further complicated by the fact that German does, indeed, use *wer* as a relative pronoun in cases in which there is no specific antecedent: *Wer nicht wagt, (der) gewinnt nichts (He who does not dare does not win)*. Similarly, *was* is used if the relative pronoun refers to an indefinite or nonexpressed antecedent: *Das ist alles (das beste), was man tun kann; Was da vorgeht, verstehe ich nicht (That is all [the best] one can do; I do not understand what is happening)*.

In other words, the relative clauses with indefinite antecedent use the interrogative pronouns as relative pronouns and can be explained as transformations of direct questions into indirect questions: *Wer hat recht? ≠ Wer recht hat [weiss ich nicht]; Was soll das bedeuten? ≠ Ich verstehe nicht, was das bedeuten soll*.

The structural explanation for adjectival clauses implies the teaching device to be used in their drill and presentation: the student can be asked to combine sentences in which the same noun occurs:

Mein Freund ist Deutschlehrer. Ich sah [meinen Freund] gestern abend.

Combination:
Mein Freund, [den] ich gestern abend sah, ist Deutschlehrer.

or

Mein Freund ist Deutschlehrer. Ich gab [meinem Freund] das Buch.
Mein Freund, [dem] ich das Buch gab, ist Deutschlehrer.

Adjectival clauses with the genitive of the relative pronoun (*dessen, deren*) are best derived from main clauses containing possessive adjectives:

Mein Freund ist Deutschlehrer. Ich kenne [seine] Mutter sehr gut.
Mein Freund, [dessen] Mutter ich sehr gut kenne, ist Deutschlehrer.

3. Adverbial Clauses

Adverbial clauses can be thought of as main clauses that have been transformed into subordinate clauses. They can then be fitted into another construction in replacement of an adverb or adverbial phrase:

Er kam zu spät [wegen des Regens]. Es regnete gestern den ganzen Tag.
Transformation: *. . . weil es gestern den ganzen Tag regnete.*
Replacement: *Er kam zu spät, [weil es gestern den ganzen Tag regnete.]*

The various types of adverbial clauses are usually grouped according to their meaning—or rather according to the meaning of the type of adverb they are replacing: clauses of cause, purpose, concession, mode, consequence, and time. The various types are fully described in most elementary grammar books. In this book, we shall concentrate on some of the major teaching problems: the "natural" exercise for the teaching and practice of the adverbial clauses is the transformation of the main clause into a subordinate one. The main clause to be transformed should be chosen in such a way that its meaning clearly indicates the type of adverbial clause (for instance, cause, purpose, time) that is required:

Robert will zu Hause bleiben. Er ist sehr müde.
Robert will zu Hause bleiben, weil er sehr müde ist.
Robert arbeitet schwer. Er will, dass seine Eltern sich freuen.
Robert arbeitet schwer, damit seine Eltern sich freuen.
Robert ist sehr müde. Aber er arbeitet noch immer.
Obgleich Robert sehr müde ist, arbeitet er noch immer.
Ich kam gestern in Berlin an. Es regnete sehr.
Als ich gestern in Berlin ankam, regnete es sehr. (Note the use of *als*, not
    wenn, for a single past event.)
Er sprach so laut. Jeder konnte ihn verstehen.
Er sprach so laut, dass jeder ihn verstehen konnte.

The grammatical problems to be watched with this kind of exercise are first of all the "*Endstellung*" of the finite verb in the subordinate clause, and second the <u>verb</u> + <u>subject</u> order in the main clause if the subordinate clause precedes. Since in the latter case, the subordinate clause really replaces an adverb that took the initial position of the main clause, the finite verb, standing in the second place of the original main clause, follows the subordinate clause immediately:

> [*Gestern*] *war ich sehr traurig.*
> [*Als ich das hörte,*] *war ich sehr traurig.*

From the syntactical point of view, the most difficult adverbial clauses are likely to be the contrary-to-fact conditional clause and certain types of concessive clauses. The contrary-to-fact conditional clauses require tenses that have no real counterpart in English, namely, the various forms of the subjunctive II according to the following scheme:

	If Clause	*Main Clause*
Present:	Subj. II	Subj. II
		(or Fut. Subj. II)
	Wenn ich das Geld hätte,	*ginge ich nach Wien.*
		(*würde ich nach Wien gehen.*)

Past: Past Subj. II.   Past Subj. II
                                                          (or Fut. Perf. Subj. II)
              Wenn ich das Geld gehabt
                    hätte,   *wäre ich nach Wien gefahren.*
                                                    (*würde ich nach Wien gefahren sein.*)
Past
Present: Past Subj. II   Subj. II
                                                          (or Fut. Subj. II)
              Wenn ich das Geld gehabt
                    hätte,   *wäre ich jetzt nicht hier.*
                                                    (*würde ich jetzt nicht hier sein.*)

Various combination exercises may be used to drill the above types of sentences:

Ich habe kein Geld. Ich bin unglücklich.
Wenn ich Geld hätte, wäre ich glücklich.
Ich habe Angst. Ich bleibe nicht hier.
Wenn ich keine Angst hätte, würde ich hier bleiben.

Transformation of "real" conditional clauses into the contrary-to-fact type may be drilled in exercises such as the following:

Wenn ich Geld habe, bin ich glücklich.
Wenn ich Geld hätte, wäre ich glücklich.

Chain drills are another effective way of drilling conditional clauses. Each student turns the main clause of the sentence produced by the student ahead of him into a subordinate clause and adds a main clause of his own:

(a) *Wenn ich Geld hätte, würde ich viele Freunde haben.*
(b) *Wenn ich viele Freunde hätte, würde ich jeden Abend ausgehen.*
(c) *Wenn ich jeden Abend ausginge, würde ich mein Geld ausgeben.*
(d) *Wenn ich mein Geld ausgäbe . . .*

A syntactical difficulty the *if*-clause shares with certain concessive types is the possibility of forming the clause without conjunction by putting the finite verb in the initial position:

Hat er Geld, (so) ist er glücklich.
Hätte er Geld, (so) wäre er glücklich.

Similarly in the concessive type:

Ist die Lage auch gefährlich, (so) müssen wir dennoch zuversichtlich sein.

or

Mag die Lage auch noch so gefährlich sein, so müssen . . .

The verb-initial subordinate clause is not very frequent in spoken German, and there is probably no real necessity for teaching its active production for either the speaking or the writing skill. However, the student should be trained to recognize this kind of construction. This can be done by various types of exercises, for example, asking the student to transform the verb-first type into clauses introduced by conjunctions:

Hätte ich Geld, so würde ich trotzdem nicht glücklich sein . . .
Wenn ich Geld hätte . . .

The other major problem connected with the formation of subordinate adverbial clauses we already mentioned in our discussion of replacement operations. English requires no change of word order, depending on the subordinating or co-ordinating nature of the clause: *I am happy because I have friends . . . for I have friends.* Nor does the use of an adverb in place of a conjunction bring about a word-order change: *Fortunately I have friends.*

In German the subordinating conjunction requires the finite verb in last position: *weil ich Freunde habe.* The co-ordinating conjunction does not influence word order because it is syntactically a link between two sentences and not part of either one: *aber ich habe Freunde.*

The adverb that is part of the sentence requires the subject to move after the verb: *trotzdem habe ich viele Freunde.* The native speaker of English is sensitive neither to the changes in word order nor to the particular kind of word categories by which it is caused. It is therefore necessary to contrast expressly both types of conjunctions and adverbs, especially if they seem to have related meanings, for example, *weil, da* (subord. conj.); *denn* (co-ord. conj.); *deshalb, darum, also,* etc. (adverbs); or *obgleich, trotzdem, obwohl* (subord. conj.); *aber* (co-ord. conj.); *dennoch, nichtsdestoweniger,* etc. (adverb). Exercises can take the form of combination drills in which the student is asked to use the word suggested by the teacher:

TEACHER: *Ich freue mich. Ich habe viele Freunde.   . . . weil*

STUDENT: *Ich freue mich, weil ich viele Freunde habe.*

TEACHER: *Ich lerne deutsch. Ich habe viele Freunde in Deutschland.*
    . . . denn

STUDENT: *Ich lerne deutsch, denn ich habe viele Freunde in Deutschland.*

TEACHER: *Ich lerne deutsch. Ich habe viele Freunde in Deutschland.*
    . . . deshalb

STUDENT: *Ich lerne deutch; deshalb habe ich viele Freunde in Deutschland.*

Another problem connected with the adverbial clause transformation arises from the possible confusion of conjunctions with prepositions. In some cases English does distinguish prepositions from conjunctions: *while he was in Vienna,* but *during his stay in Vienna;* in other cases it does not: *after he came back from Vienna, after his stay in Vienna.* In German the situation is similar; but, unfortunately, the cases in which there is no distinction between the preposition and conjunction do not overlap: *nachdem er von Wien zurückkehrte,* but *nach seinem Aufenthalt in Wien.* In a similar way: *weil er krank war, wegen seiner Krankheit* (English *because, because of*); *seitdem er zurückgekehrt ist, seit seiner Rückkehr* (*since, since*); *bevor er zurückkehrt, vor seiner Rückkehr* (*before, before*); and so forth. In cases such as these, the prepositions and conjunctions are best contrasted in exercises that may take various forms, for example, replacement of a prepositional phrase or clause:

Karl muss wegen seiner Krankheit hierbleiben.
Karl muss hierbleiben, weil er krank ist.

Seit seiner Rückkehr spricht er nicht mehr mit mir.
Seitdem er zurückgekehrt ist, spricht er nicht mehr mit mir.

In some instances the German type of conjunction may be in direct conflict with English, which employs a construction that if directly imitated by the pupil will lead to impossible German. The German equivalent of *The more he works, the less he knows* precludes the use of the definite article: *Je mehr er arbeitet, desto weniger weiss er.* Or: *He speaks as if he knew the truth, Er spricht, als ob er die Wahrheit wüsste* (*als ob*, not *als *wenn*). Sentences of this type can be drilled in replacement exercises:

TEACHER: *Er spricht, als ob er die Wahrheit wüsste.*

TEACHER: _____ *antwortet* _____ .

STUDENT: *Er antwortet, als ob er die Wahrheit wüsste.*

TEACHER: _____ *den Grund* _____ .

STUDENT: *Er antwortet, als ob er den Grund wüsste.*

Just as in other cases in which it is necessary to impress upon the student that he must avoid a direct imitation of an English construction, we can also use pattern drills cued by English in order to create an overt awareness of the English-German contrast:

The more he earns, the more he has.
Je mehr er verdient, desto mehr hat er.

The earlier he comes, the later he leaves.
Je früher er kommt, desto später geht er weg.

Some difficulties connected with the use of conjunctions are caused by vocabulary problems of the type to be discussed in the next chapter. Perhaps the most obvious of those is the German use of *als* and *wenn*, which clearly divides the field of meaning covered by English *when*, requiring the use of *als* whenever the subordinate clause describes a **single**, **simple past action**:

When(ever) I come to Berlin, I see all my friends.
Wenn ich nach Berlin komme . . .
                    but
Yesterday when I came to Berlin . . .
Als ich gestern nach Berlin kam . . .

CHAPTER VIII

Problems of Meaning and Vocabulary

(A) IDIOMS AND DIFFICULT CONSTRUCTION TYPES

From the point of view of English, any German construction that differs markedly from English speech habits may be called idiomatic. If the word "**idiomatic**" is used in this rather loose sense, more than 50 per cent of German is idiomatic. A somewhat more precise, linguistic definition is to consider an idiom any expression which has a meaning that cannot be arrived at from the meaning of its component parts. Thus, taking the literal meaning of *haben* and *Pech* (*pitch*) it is not possible to predict that *Pech haben* means *to have bad luck;* or analyzing the meaning of *führen* (*lead*), and *Schild* (*shield*) it is difficult to predict that *Er führt nichts Gutes im Schild* means *He has bad intentions* or *He is up to no good* (to quote an English idiom). Idioms of this type must—almost by definition—be memorized and learned as units.

In a somewhat different category are expressions—also commonly and popularly classified as idioms—which simply represent a construction type not used in English for expressing the same meaning: the meaning of *Ich habe das Mädchen sehr gern* or *Das Mädchen gefällt mir* is not unpredictable according to the elements of the construction. It is the construction itself that causes the trouble. The student equating *gefallen* with *like* may translate *I like* with *ich gefalle* and come up with either an impossible sentence or one that confuses the subject-object relation: *Ich gefalle dem Mädchen* (*I am pleasing to the girl/The girl likes me*). Idioms and difficult construction types must be carefully explained and drilled in replacement or simple transformation exercises:

153

Hat das Mädchen Ihnen gefallen?   *Ja, sie hat mir gefallen.*
Hat die Vorstellung dem Lehrer   *Ja, sie hat ihm gefallen.*
    gefallen?

or

Diese Entscheidung geht meine
    Eltern nichts an.
(This decision is none of my
    parents' business.)
    . . . Antwort   *Diese Antwort geht meine Eltern*
       nichts an.
    . . . Brief   *Dieser Brief geht meine Eltern*
       nichts an.
    . . . meinen Bruder (mein Bruder)   *Dieser Brief geht meinen Bruder*
       nichts an.

(B) SIGNIFIER INTERFERENCE

As we have stated earlier, any linguistic unit from the morpheme level up is composed of a material part of the sounds that make up the "signifier," and of a meaning, a "signified" with which the sounds are connected. Vocabulary problems can have their origin in the meaning part of the word, or they can originate in the signifier, the sounds themselves. The trouble caused by the signifier is usually some sort of confusion. Basically the confusion can be of two types: a word can be confused with an English word that sounds very much like it or at least similar, or it can be confused with an identical or very similar German word.

Confusion with a similar or almost identical English word leads us to a brief consideration of the so-called "false friends." Obviously there are many cases in which English and German words are nearly alike and in which the similarity in form corresponds to a similarity or identity in meaning: *Hand/hand, Finger/finger, bringen/bring, Knie/knee, Fuss/foot,* and so on. It is this very similarity in meaning and form that makes the cases in which similarity in form is **not** accompanied by similarity in meaning doubly difficult to combat. To give a few examples of false friends: *become ≠ bekommen, Dose ≠ dosis, exerzieren ≠ exercise, brav ≠ brave.* In some instances there may be a partial overlap between the meaning of the English and the corresponding German word: German *Lust* and English *lust* can at times overlap in the meaning of "sensual appetite," but in the vast majority of possible uses, German *Lust* simply means pleasure or desire: *Ich habe Lust, ins Kino zu gehen* (*I feel like going to the movies*).

Cases of false friends must be carefully pointed out to the student, and the correct usage should be practiced in exercises that contrast the correct German usage of the false friend as well as the real German equivalent of the English counterpart:

> *Die Kinder waren brav. Sie machten ihre Aufgabe.*
>
> but
>
> *Die Soldaten waren tapfer; sie hielten ihre Stellung.*

Confusion of German words with other German words can also cause considerable trouble. German has a substantial number of verbs that either are or sound nearly alike. In some cases the similarity is due to an actual historical relationship, in other cases it is fortuitous. In any case there is the possibility that the student may either use the wrong form or attach the wrong meaning to the form he hears or sees. To give examples of some verbs that may be confused because of their similarity: *stehlen, stellen; wiegen,* past *wiegte; wiegen,* past *wog; kennen, können; denken, danken; liegen, legen; mahlen, malen; bieten, bitten, beten.* Confusion in meaning or usage may also occur with separable and nonseparable verbs that are in the infinite distinguished only by the placement of the primary stress accent: *'wiederholen, wieder'holen; 'umfahren, um'fahren; 'übertreten, über'treten* (for example, *Er ist zur republikanischen Partei übergetreten; Er hat alle Gesetze übertreten*).

Also a considerable number of pairs of nouns are either identical or nearly identical. Sometimes the members of the pair are distinguished only by the plural forms: *die Bank, die Bänke* (*bench*) ≠ *die Bank, die Banken* (*bank*); *das Wort, die Wörter* ≠ *das Wort, die Worte* (referring to connected speech). In some instances the distinction concerns gender as well as plural formation: *das Band, die Bänder* (*ribbon*) ≠ *der Band, die Bände* (*volume, book*); *der Leiter, die Leiter* (*leader*) ≠ *die Leiter, die Leitern* (*ladder*); *der Tor, die Toren* (*fool*) ≠ *das Tor, die Tore* (*door, entrance*). In a few cases the only distinction is either in the absence of a plural form or just in the gender: *der Erbe, die Erben* (*heir*) ≠ *das Erbe* (*inheritance*), *der Hut, die Hüte* (*hat*) ≠ *die Hut* (*protection*); *der See, die Seen* (*lake*) ≠ *die See*, but *der Heide, die Heiden* (*pagan*) ≠ *die Heide, die Heiden* (*heather, heath*).

If necessary, similar nouns and verbs should be contrasted in sentences illustrating their exact meaning, and the student should be asked to make up sentences of his own to illustrate the usage of the confusing pair. We should emphasize here that having the student make up illustrative examples according to a model is a far more effective way to deal with the problem than having him memorize or repeat sample sentences—a procedure which will not necessarily clear up the confusion existing in the student's mind, but may very well serve to aggravate it even further.

(C) PROBLEMS OF MEANING

No word in any language can truly be said to "mean" a word in another language. As we have stated in Chapter 1, building stones of different systems are not identical. The student who establishes the equation English x = German y, either as the result of learning a vocabulary list or as the result of remembering a sentence, may make any number of errors if he applies this equation in situations in which it is simply not valid. The best advice we can give the student is to tell him that the equation between a German and an English word is most likely to hold true in the new situation if the latter resembles closely the situation in which this equation was established in the first place. The advice also implies that memorizing words from a vocabulary list and without context is a fairly poor way of acquiring vocabulary because an equation of, let us say, the type *leave/verlassen* does not provide any situational context whatsoever and therefore provides no means of judging under what circumstances this equation is likely to hold true. If the equation has been established through a sentence, such as *Ich verlasse Deutschland, I am leaving Germany*, some context for extension has been provided. *I am leaving Paris, I am leaving the room* look like fairly safe possibilities for extending the equation *leave/verlassen*. The general meaning and the grammatical constructions involved are quite similar to those in the original situation. *I am leaving* (no object) changes the grammatical construction—and indeed the equation no longer applies: *Ich gehe weg* (*verlassen* necessitates an object). *I am leaving my friends behind, I left the book in the classroom* change the meaning from "getting away from a place" to "leaving something in a place"; "leaving" is now expressed by *zurücklassen* or *lassen*.

The most important and frequent cases in which an English concept is split up into two or several German concepts should be expressly pointed out and drilled. Examples are numerous, for instance, *time*:

What time is it?	*Wie spät ist es?*
	(*Wieviel Uhr ist es?*)
I have not any time.	*Ich habe keine Zeit.*
I saw him five times.	*Ich sah ihn fünfmal.*

The problem of teaching the corresponding German concepts becomes increasingly difficult as the conceptual differences involved in the distinction made by German seem fuzzy and unclear to the speaker of English. To give an example, German makes a distinction between location, motion toward the speaker (*woher*), and motion away from the speaker (*wohin*). English makes no such compulsory distinction: *Where are you? Where are you going?* and so forth. Thus on the basis of an equation *where = wo* the student may produce such a non-German sentence as **Wo gehst du heute abend?* (instead of *wohin*).

At the same time, however, the teaching problem is not formidable because the conceptual difference between location, motion to, and motion from is clear to the speaker of English. It is not compulsory in his language, but it can be made (*where* vs. *where to*, *where from*).

To teach the difference between *kennen* and *wissen* or *du* and *Sie* represents a quite different and more serious problem. Here German makes a distinction that does not exist in English. In such cases an attempt must be made to explain the German concept to the student. (Ultimately the precise concept can be created only by a great deal of practice, which allows the student to see the exact common denominator of all situations in which the concept is used.) In the case of *du* vs. *Sie*, the situations in which *du* may be used must be pointed out: addressing children (up to about fourteen years), close friends, relatives, and animals. In the case of *kennen* vs. *wissen*, we can partly rely on purely grammatical areas: only *wissen* can precede a subordinate noun clause (*ich weiss, dass, wo*, and so on). *Kennen* requires a direct object. These rules serve to narrow the area in which the student must rely on the recognition of a conceptual difference: *kennen* alone may be used in reference to persons; it really means "to be acquainted with" and is used to express the kind of "knowing" that can be achieved by just looking at something once.

Practice in the creation and use of a new conceptual difference takes best the form of exercises in which the student is forced to make the choice between alternative expressions. A sentence like *Ich kenne Herrn Schmidt* can be taken as the starting point. Then the student is asked to use *kenne* vs. *weiss* according to the substitution suggested for the object:

. . . *wo Herr Schmidt ist*	*Ich weiss, wo Herr Schmidt ist.*
. . . *seinen Freund*	*Ich kenne seinen Freund.*
. . . *Paris*	*Ich kenne Paris.*
. . . (nothing)	*Ich weiss.*

In cases in which either *kenne* or *weiss* may be used, as in *Ich kenne die Antwort* ≠ *Ich weiss die Antwort*, this kind of exercise reaches the limits of its usefulness. The appreciation and correct use of *kenne* vs. *weiss* depends then on the knowledge of the conceptual difference, not on clear-cut contextual or grammatical cues.

The problem of having to learn a conceptual difference that is foreign to English occurs not only with vocabulary but also in cases of choice between grammatical form. The best examples of this are furnished by the subjunctive and the German past tenses. Which subjunctive has to be used is in some cases clearly dictated by grammatical rule. The contrary-to-fact conditional sentence uses subjunctive II, *wenn ich Zeit hätte.* The third person imperative, or "optative," uses subjunctive I, *Lang lebe der König* (*Long live the King*). But when it comes to the use of the subjunctive in the indirect discourse, the situation is more complicated.

The difference in meaning between subjunctive I and subjunctive II is that the latter seems to indicate even further remoteness from reality than the former. The speaker of German can use the indicatives or the subjunctives to specify his attitude toward the events reported in the indirect discourse. Use of the indicative reveals that the speaker has reasonable confidence about the veracity of the events which he is reporting: *Karl sagt, dass sein Bruder die Antwort weiss.* The use of subjunctive I shows that the speaker feels neutral concerning the accuracy and veracity of the events: *Karl sagt, dass sein Bruder die Antwort wisse.* The use of subjunctive II suggests skepticism or disbelief: *Karl sagt, dass sein Bruder die Antwort wüsste.* In all cases in which indicative and subjunctive are identical (1st person and 3rd person plural, present, and subjunctive I; past tense and subjunctive II of weak verb), the forms of subjunctive II are used in indirect discourse if a subjunctive is required: *Er sagt, dass Sie die Antwort wüssten* (rather than *wissen*); *Er sagt, dass Sie Ihre Aufgaben machten.* Whenever possible the future subjunctive II (conditional) may be used to indicate the speaker's lack of confidence in the veracity of the reported events: *Er sagte, dass Sie Ihre Aufgaben machen würden.* English lacks the possibility of indicating the speaker's attitude by choosing a special verb form in the indirect cause. A sentence like *Karl sagt, dass er die Antwort wüsste* would thus have to be rendered by something like *Karl pretends he knows the answer* or *Karl says he knows the answer* (heavy stress on *says*). A similar way of conveying the speaker's attitude toward the veracity of events would probably also be used in most levels of spoken German, in which the subjunctive—though flourishing in the written form of the language—is quite rare as the medium of expression in indirect discourse.

The student's correct use and understanding of the German past tenses (past, present perfect) must be based on a clear recognition of the peculiarities of the English usage. His normal tendency will be to equate the English past with the German past (or imperfect), *Ich sprach/I spoke*, and the English present perfect with the German perfect, *Ich habe gesprochen/I have spoken*. Unfortunately, this equation is an erroneous one; neither is the terminology used in many grammar books— either English or German—very fortunate, since names like "imperfect" or "past perfect" do not fully or adequately describe the meaning of the tenses. Purely descriptive terms such as "simple past" and "compound past" or "first past" and "second past" are, in many ways, less misleading. English has a simple past tense to denote a simple completed past action: *Yesterday I spoke with my friend*. This simple past may be rendered in German by either the simple or the compound past: *Gestern sprach ich mit meinem Freund; Gestern habe ich mit meinem Freund gesprochen*. The choice of either the one or the other is a matter of style. In colloquial German the simple past has become rare and is often felt to be unnatural and stilted.

The English compound past is really a past indefinite or present perfect: *Have you read this book by Thomas Mann?* implies that the exact time when the reading took place is not relevant. The expected answer is, *Yes, I have read it* or *No I haven't read it;* but note that the speaker of English will switch to the simple past as soon as definite time reference is introduced: *Yes, I read it two years ago* (not *have read*). Another implication of the compound past is that it describes an action that somehow still affects the present: *I have read the book* implies that **I am now** a person who has read the book at some **indefinite** time in the past. *I have been in Paris* means that I am **now** a person who at some time in the past has been in Paris. The German compound past or present perfect is used in a similar way: *Haben Sie das Buch von Thomas Mann(schon) gelesen?, Sind Sie (je, schon) in Paris gewesen?* In instances in which English would quite definitely use the compound past, the same tense should be used in German. The simple and compound past of German are thus not always exchangeable according to purely stylistic levels.

An additional complication is introduced by the English progressive tense. Of course, it is simple enough to tell the student that the *be + ing*-form tenses of English have no German counterpart: *I am speaking ≠ Ich spreche, I was speaking ≠ Ich sprach*. Unfortunately, the problem does not end there. English has a past progressive, *I have been speaking*, which indicates that the action began in the past and continues into the present. For any such action, German uses the present tense and the student must learn to resist the temptation to use a past tense: *I have been working for two hours* ≠ *Ich arbeite seit zwei Stunden*. It would be easy if the student could be told categorically that in such cases the English *-ing* form signals the necessity of using the German present tense. However, English has a number of rather frequent verbs that do not admit the *-ing* form or only in very special cases: *be, know, understand*. With those verbs the compound past, or past perfect, is used to denote the past action continuing into the present: *I have known this for many years; I have been here for two hours.* In all such cases, the German equivalent of the present perfect is the present tense: *Ich weiss das schon seit vielen Jahren; Ich bin schon seit zwei Stunden hier.*

For a verb like *to be* we can thus set up the following German-English equivalents:

1. *I was in Paris last summer.*   *Letzten Sommer war ich in Paris.*
    Letzten Sommer bin ich in Paris gewesen.
2. *Have you ever been in Paris?*   *Sind Sie je in Paris gewesen?*
3. *I have been here since two o'clock.*   *Ich bin schon seit zwei Uhr hier.*

The salient facts to be grasped by the student are therefore the following:

1.   He may use the simple past or the present perfect (compound past) in instances in which he would use the simple past in English;

2.   If the compound past is required in English, it is also used in German; but—

3.   Any action that is still going on in the present must be described in the present tense.

Intellectual grasp of these facts may not be enough. Especially with verbs in which the absence of an English progressive tense brings about the equation English compound past = German present, German sentences using the present tense should be drilled extensively in question-and-answer drills or in response to English cues.

(D) GENERAL PROBLEMS IN TEACHING VOCABULARY

Certain aspects of teaching meaning and vocabulary have been the subject of perennial discussion among methodologists. What words are to be taught? How is the meaning to be conveyed to the student?

The question of what words are to be taught has led to the establishment of various types of frequency lists and frequency studies. In considering the value of such frequency studies, various factors must be taken into account. First, we must keep in mind the fundamental difference between function words (the words that form part of the structure or pattern) and the nouns, adverbs, verbs, and adjectives. Function words are likely to appear very frequently in any sort of German, regardless of the nature of the sample. When it comes to the nouns, adverbs, adjectives, and verbs, the frequency with which they appear is very largely determined by the sample. One of the main objections that has been raised against frequency counts is that once we go beyond the function-word dominated range of the first few hundred, successive samples taken from different types of speech or writing show quite divergent frequencies for the same word. This is another way of saying that the question of what words to teach must ultimately depend on the purposes and aims of the course. If the aim is to make nineteenth-century literature accessible to the student, then a frequency count based on nineteenth-century literature will furnish valuable guide lines to the course. For the student whose aim is the reading of technical material in a field of engineering, the same frequency list will prove of little value.

Another possible approach to vocabulary frequency is the one used in the construction of basic English and the German method based on the same general principle ("German through Pictures"). There the words included are not those determined by a frequency count but those judged necessary to express essential concepts (which in turn can be used to express other concepts). Greatest possible economy is the goal. Hence all possible synonyms are avoided, as are vocabulary items that can be adequately expressed in other terms. Therefore, quite unlike the objective count of either spoken or written materials, words are included in the frequency list on the basis of a subjective judgment of their usefulness.

The so-called empirical approach to frequency studies is in a sense a combination of the subjunctive and objective approach. The frequency list is based on the objective investigation of frequency in a large number of samples, but the choice of the samples is ultimately based on a subjunctive judgment. The frequency list, then, includes not only a frequency rating for each word but also a range—a figure indicating in how many of the samples the word was found. The most modern, scientific, and up-to-date frequency study of German ("*Grunddeutsch*") is basically a study of this type. It is based on a wide variety of samples and includes information as to frequency and range—and beyond that also an indication of the semantic range (the English equivalents) of the words found in the list. Of course, no frequency list can solve the problem of divergent purposes for the individual student, but books based on the *"Grunddeutsch"* frequency count may at least give the optimal base from which to branch out into different specific areas of the German *"Wortschatz."*

We have already indicated our opposition to learning meanings from a vocabulary list without the context of specific situation and utterances. There are, however, a few learning situations in which the use of vocabulary lists may be justified. A student interested in reading materials in a specific technical field can be given a vocabulary list adapted to his special field of interest. Since he is interested only in passive recognition, and since the concepts involved are well known and well defined, a technical vocabulary list may prove very useful to him. Even in a course oriented toward active production of German, vocabulary lists associated with a specific semantic field or specific area of experience may be useful, for example, lists of words associated with auto racing, football, travel, or means of transportation. The fact that each vocabulary item on the list is associated with a specific area of experience and meaning narrows its range so that misunderstanding or misapplications are unlikely; for instance, the equation *Kühler/radiator* may be quite misleading, unless it is found in a vocabulary list specifically dealing with automobiles. The topically oriented vocabulary list can, in turn, be used to encourage the student to employ the various sentence-creation operations so that he forms sentences or paragraphs dealing with specific areas of experience or of particular interest to him.

Many teachers prefer a method of explaining vocabulary through German to the giving of English equivalents. This explaining in German can take the form of providing synonyms (*dauern/während*) or antonyms (*schwarz ≠ weiss, klein ≠ gross*) or of actual explanation (*Apotheke: ein Geschaäft in dem man Arzneien verkauft*). There is undoubtedly a great advantage to staying within German. In the equation or association *weiss = white*, one member of the association (*white*) is useless from the point of view of the German student and teacher; but association of German with German will increase the student's vocabulary. The only possible dangers of staying within German at all costs are that at times the German explanations may become too complicated or uneconomical, and that exact synonyms and really accurate explanations may not be available. It is then up to the teacher to decide at which point the simple English equivalent may not be preferable after all.

Intimately connected with the learning of vocabulary is the problem of the cultural context and environment in which the words function. The more dissimilar this cultural environment from the American cultural scene is, the more misleading is the implied or overt equivalence of German and American vocabulary. The author of this book has spent a considerable time of his life in German and American high schools and universities. At times he was faced with the necessity of finding German equivalents for "high school graduation," "senior," "department head," "department meeting," "principal," etc., or English equivalents for "*Abitur*," "*Reifeprüfung*," "*Colloquium*," "*Seminar*," etc. Whatever the equivalent, it implied a falsification of either the German or the English vocabulary item.

Ultimately, words have meaning only in a particular cultural context, and the real grasp of their meaning depends not on the substitution of an equivalent meaning in the native language but on an understanding of the culture in which they normally function. It is for this reason that language study and the comprehension of culture must be intimately and inevitably linked.

BIBLIOGRAPHY

Bibliography

The bibliography does not aim to be exhaustive. It attempts to list a series of books that may serve as useful outside reading and present in greater detail some of the material dealt with in this book. With very few exceptions, the bibliography does not list periodical articles. The symbol (R) after a reference indicates that it is particularly recommended. Books marked with (R) either contain documentation or additional reading supplementing individual chapters of this text. For further bibliographical references the reader may consult the bibliographies contained in books marked by the symbol (B). The asterisks used with the titles are an indication of their level of difficulty and of the degree of technical knowledge they either presuppose or attempt to impart. Two asterisks are reserved for the most technical works, of importance only to the reader with special interest in linguistics. Books that do not presuppose a technical knowledge beyond linguistics and that do not aim at imparting a technical knowledge beyond the minimum needed for the application of linguistics in the classroom do not carry any marking.

Theoretical Foundations (General Linguistics, Phonetics, Psychology)

**BACH, EMMON. *An Introduction to Transformational Grammar*. New York: Holt, Rinehart and Winston, 1964.

BELYAYEV, B. V. *The Psychology of Teaching Foreign Languages*. Translated by Dr. R. F. HINGLEY. New York: The Macmillan Company, 1964.

*BLOCH, BERNARD, and TRAGER, GEORGE. *Outline of Linguistic Analysis*. Baltimore: Linguistic Society of America, 1942 (reprinted in 1950).

*BLOOMFIELD, LEONARD. *Language*. New York: Henry Holt & Company, 1945.

CARROLL, JOHN B. *The Study of Language*. Cambridge, Mass.: Harvard University Press, 1953. (R)

————. "Research on Teaching Foreign Languages" in NATHANIEL L. GAGE, *Handbook of Research on Teaching*. Chicago: Rand McNally & Co., 1963.

———— and SAPON, S. M. *Manual, Modern Language Aptitude Test*. New York: Psychological Corporation, 1959.

**CHOMSKY, NOAM. *Syntactic Structures*. The Hague, Paris: Mouton and Co., 1957.

————. *Aspects of the Theory of Syntax*. Cambridge, Mass.: The M.I.T. Press, 1965.

DINEEN, FRANCIS P., S.J. *An Introduction to General Linguistics*. New York: Holt, Rinehart and Winston, 1967.

*EISENSON, JON. *The Psychology of Speech*. New York: Crofts, 1946.

FERGUSON, CHARLES E. (Supervisor). *Teaching a Second Language* (Series of five films on 1. Nature of Language, 2. The Sounds of Language, 3. Organization of Language, 4. Words and Their Meanings, 5. Modern Techniques in Language Teaching), Teaching Manual to accompany film. Washington, D.C.: Center for Applied Linguistics, 1963. New York: Teaching Film Custodians, 1963.

*GLEASON, H. A., JR. *An Introduction to Descriptive Linguistics*. Revised Edition. New York: Holt, Rinehart and Winston, 1961.

*HAAS, WILLIAM, UITTI, KARL D., and WELLS, RULON. *Linguistics*. Englewood Cliffs, N.J.: Prentice-Hall, 1964.

HALL, ROBERT A., JR. *Introductory Linguistics*. Philadelphia: Chilton Company, 1964.

————. *Linguistics and Your Language*. New York: Doubleday & Company, 1960.

**HARRIS, ZELLIG S. *Structural Linguistics*. Chicago: University of Chicago Press, Phoenix Books, 1963.

*HEFFNER, R-M. S. *General Phonetics*. Madison, Wis.: University of Wisconsin Press, 1949.

*HILL, ARCHIBALD A. *Introduction to Linguistic Structures*. New York: Harcourt, Brace and Company, 1958.

*HOCKETT, CHARLES F. *A Course in Modern Linguistics*. New York: The Macmillan Company, 1958.

HOIJER, HARRI, Editor. *Language and Culture* (Conference on the Interrelations of Language and other Aspects of Culture). Chicago: University of Chicago Press, 1954.

MARTINET, ANDRÉ. *Elements of General Linguistics*. Chicago: University of Chicago Press, 1964.

————. *Eléments de linguistique générale*. Paris, France: Collection Armand Colin, 1960.

*————. *La description phonologique*. Paris-Genève: Société de publications romanes et françaises, Librairie Droz, M. J. Minard, 1956.

**OGDEN, C. K., and RICHARDS, I. A. *The Meaning of Meaning*. New York: Harcourt, Brace and Company, 1923.

ORNSTEIN, JACOB, and GAGE, WILLIAM. *The ABC's of Language and Linguistics*. Philadelphia: Chilton Company, 1964.

*OSGOOD, CHARLES, and SEBEOK, THOMAS, Editors. *Psycholinguistics, a Survey of Theory and Research Problems. Supplement to International Journal of American Linguistics*. Baltimore: Waverley Press, 1954.

PEI, MARIO. *Invitation to Linguistics, a Basic Introduction to the Science of Language*. Garden City, N.Y.: Doubleday & Company, 1965.

**PIKE, KENNETH. *Language in Relation to a Unified Theory of the Structure of Human Behavior.* Glendale, Calif.: Summer Institute of Linguistics, Part I, 1954; Part II, 1955; Part III, 1960.

**———. *Phonemics: A Technique of Reducing Languages to Writing.* Ann Arbor, Mich.: University of Michigan Press, 1947.

*———. *Phonetics: A Critical Analysis of Phonetic Theory and a Technique for the Practical Description of Sounds.* Ann Arbor, Mich.: University of Michigan Press, 1943.

*POTTER, SIMEON. *Modern Linguistics.* New York: W. W. Norton & Company, 1964.

The Principles of the International Phonetic Association, Being a Description of the International Phonetic Alphabet and the Manner of Using It. London: International Phonetic Association, 1953.

RIVERS, WILGA M. *The Psychologist and the Foreign-Language Teacher.* Chicago: University of Chicago Press, 1964. (R)

SAPIR, EDWARD. *Language: An Introduction to the Study of Speech.* New York: Harcourt, Brace and Company, 1921 (Paperback edition: Harvest Books).

*SAPORTA, SOL, Editor. *Psycholinguistics: A Book of Readings.* New York: Holt, Rinehart and Winston, 1961.

*SAUSSURE, FERDINAND DE. *Cours de linguistique générale.* Publié par Charles Bally et Albert Sechehaye avec la collaboration d'Albert Riedlinger, Paris: Payot, 1955.

*———. *Course in General Linguistics.* Translated by WADE BASKIN. New York: Philosophical Library, 1959.

SCHERER, GEORGE A. C., and WERTHEIMER, MICHAEL. *A Psychological Experiment in Foreign Language Teaching.* New York: McGraw-Hill Book Company, 1964.

*SKINNER, B. F. *Verbal Behavior.* New York: Appleton-Century-Crofts, 1957.

*WEINREICH, URIEL. *Languages in Contact.* New York: Publications of the Linguistic Circle of New York, No. 1, 1953.

*WHATMOUGH, JOSHUA. *Language, a Modern Synthesis.* London: Secker and Warburg, 1956 (Paperback, New York: Mentor Books, The New American Library, 1957).

Applied Linguistics

ALLEN, HAROLD B. *Readings in Applied English Linguistics.* New York: Appleton-Century-Crofts, 1958.

BELASCO, SIMON, Editor. *Anthology for Use with a Guide for Teachers in NDEA Language Institutes.* Boston: D. C. Heath & Company, 1961.

*BLOOMFIELD, LEONARD. *Outline Guide for the Practical Study of Foreign Languages.* Baltimore: Linguistic Society of America, 1942.

CORNELIUS, EDWIN T., JR. *Language Teaching (A Guide for Teachers of Foreign Languages).* New York: Thomas Y. Crowell Company, 1953.

FERGUSON, CHARLES A., and STEWART, WILLIAM A. *Linguistic Reading Lists for Teachers of Modern Languages.* Washington D.C.: Center for Applied Linguistics, 1963.

FRIES, CHARLES C. *Teaching and Learning English as a Foreign Language*. Ann Arbor, Mich.: University of Michigan Press, 1945.

HALL, ROBERT A., JR. *New Ways to Learn a Foreign Language*. New York: Bantam Books, Inc., 1966.

HALLIDAY, M. A. K., MCINTOSH, ANGUS, and STREVENS, PETER. *The Linguistic Sciences and Language Teaching*. Bloomington Ind.: Indiana University Press, 1965.

LADO, ROBERT. *Language Teaching: A Scientific Approach*. New York: McGraw-Hill Book Company, 1964. (R)

————. *Linguistics Across Cultures, Applied Linguistics for Language Teachers*. Ann Arbor, Mich.: University of Michigan Press, 1957. (R)

MACKEY, WILLIAM FRANCIS. *Language Teaching Analysis*. London: Longmans, Green and Company, 1965.

MARCHAND, JAMES WOODROW, and BELASCO, SIMON. *Applied Linguistics: German, a Guide for Teachers*. Boston: D. C. Heath & Company, 1961. (R)

MOULTON, WILLIAM G. *A Linguistic Guide to Language Learning*. New York: Modern Language Association of America, 1966.

PEI, MARIO. *How to Learn Languages and What Languages to Learn*. New York: Harper and Row, 1966.

POLITZER, ROBERT L. *Foreign Language Learning—A Linguistic Introduction*. Englewood Cliffs, N.J.: Prentice-Hall, 1965.

General Methodology, Classroom and Laboratory Techniques

"What Do We Know about Teaching Modern Foreign Languages?" *Audio Visual Instruction*, Vol. 4, No. 6 (September 1959). National Education Association, Department of Audio Visual Instruction.
   Entire volume is devoted to language instruction, laboratory equipment, and techniques.

BROOKS, NELSON. *Language and Language Learning, Theory and Practice*. Second Edition. New York: Harcourt, Brace & World, 1964. (R)

CAPRETZ, PIERRE J. (Project Director). *Audio Lingual Techniques for Teaching Foreign Languages* (includes a 60-minute film on the teaching of French). Washington, D.C.: Norwood Films, 1963.

COCHRAN, ANNE. *Modern Methods of Teaching English as a Foreign Language: A guide to modern materials with particular reference to the Far East*. Washington, D.C.: Educational Service, 1954.

COUNCIL OF CHIEF STATE SCHOOL OFFICERS. *Purchase Guide (for programs in science, mathematics, foreign languages)*. Boston: Ginn and Company, 1959.

FINN, JAMES D., and PERRIN, DONALD G. *Teaching Machines and Programed Learning, a Survey of the Industry—1962*. Washington, D.C.: U.S. Department of Health, Education, and Welfare. Office of Education, Contract No. OE-34019, 1962.

Foreign Language Laboratory Techniques. Supplement of Louisiana Foreign Language Teachers Association News Letter. Baton Rouge, 1956. (R)

French for Secondary Schools. Albany: New York State Education Department, 1960. (R)

HAGBOLDT, PETER. *The Teaching of German*. Boston: D. C. Heath & Company, 1940.

HIRSCH, RUTH. *Audio-Visual Aids in Language Teaching* (Monograph Series on Languages and Linguistics, No. 5). Washington, D.C.: The Institute of Language and Linguistics, School of Foreign Service, Georgetown University, 1954.

HOCKING, ELTON. *Language Laboratory and Language Learning*. Washington, D.C.: Department of Audio-Visual Instruction, National Education Association of the United States, Monograph 2, 1964.

HUEBNER, THEODORE. *Audio-Visual Techniques in Teaching Foreign Languages, a Practical Handbook*. New York: New York University Press, 1960.

———. *How to Teach Foreign Languages Effectively*. New York: New York University Press, 1959.

HUTCHINSON, JOSEPH C. *Modern Foreign Languages in High School: The Language Laboratory*. Washington, D.C.: Office of Education, 1961.

JESPERSON, OTTO. *How to Teach a Foreign Language*. New York: The Macmillan Company, 1904.

JODICE, DON R. *Guidelines to Language Teaching in Classroom and Laboratory*. Washington, D.C.: Electronic Teaching Laboratories, 1961.

JOHNSTON, MARJORIE C., and SEERLEY, CATHERINE C. *Foreign Language Laboratories in Schools and Colleges*. Washington, D.C.: U.S. Department of Health Education, and Welfare, Bulletin 1959, No. 3.

KONE, ELLIOT H., Editor. *Language Laboratories—Modern Techniques in Teaching Foreign Languages*. New York: Bulletin of the Connecticut Audio-Visual Education Association, Vol. 19, 1959–60.

LADO, ROBERT. *Language Testing. The Construction and Use of Foreign Language Tests, a Teacher's Book*. London: Longmans, Green & Company, 1961; New York: McGraw-Hill Book Company, Inc., 1964. (R)

LÉON, P. R., *Laboratoire de langues et correction phonétique, Essai méthodologique*. Paris: Didier, 1962.

MARTY, FERNAND L. *Language Laboratory Learning*. Wellesley, Mass.: Audio-Visual Publications, 1960. (R)

———. *Programming a Basic Foreign Language Course: Prospects for Self-Instruction*. Hollins, Va.: Audio-Visual Publications, 1962.

MÉRAS, EDMOND A. *A Language Teacher's Guide*. Second Edition. New York: Harper & Row, 1962. (R)

MICHEL, JOSEPH, Editor. *Foreign Language Teaching, An Anthology*. New York: The Macmillan Company, 1967.

MORTON, R. "The Language Laboratory as a Teaching Machine," *International Journal of American Linguistics XXVI* (1960), 113–166.

NEWMARK, MAXIM, Editor. *Twentieth Century Modern Language Teaching*. New York: Philosophical Library, 1948.

NOSTRAND, HOWARD LEE, *et al. Research on Language Teaching: An Annotated International Bibliography for 1945–1964*. Second Edition, revised. Seattle and London: University of Washington Press, 1965.

O'CONNOR, PATRICIA. *Modern Foreign Languages in High School: Pre-reading Instruction*. Washington, D.C.: Contract No. OE-2700. Bulletin 1960, No. 9.

OLLMAN, J., Editor. *Selective List of Materials.* New York: Modern Language Association, 1962. (R)

O'ROURKE, EVERETT V. *et al. French, Listening, Speaking, Reading, Writing.* Sacramento, Calif.: California State Department of Education, 1962. (R)

POLITZER, ROBERT L. *et al. Performance Criteria for Foreign Language Teachers.* Stanford, Calif.: Center for Research and Development in Teaching, Stanford University, 1966.

QUILTER, DANIEL E. *Do's and Don't's in Audio-Visual Teaching.* Waltham, Mass.: Blaisdell Publishing Company, 1966.

STACK, EDWARD M. *The Language Laboratory and Modern Language Teaching.* Second Edition. New York: Oxford University Press, 1966. (R)

VALDMAN, ALBERT, Editor. *Trends in Language Teaching.* New York: McGraw Hill Book Company, 1966.

VALETTE, REBECCA M. *Modern Language Testing.* New York: Harcourt, Brace and World, Inc., 1967.

WALSH, DONALD D. *What's What: A List of Useful Terms for the Teacher of Modern Languages.* New York: The Modern Language Association of America, 1963.

German Phonetics, Teaching of Pronunciation

BRANDENSTEIN, W. *Einführung in die Phonetik und Phonologie.* Vienna, Austria: Gerold Verlag, 1950.

DE BOOR, HELMUT, and DIELS, PAUL, Editors. *Theodor Siebs: Deutsche Hochsprache.* Sixteenth Edition. Berlin, Germany: W. de Gruyten Verlag, 1957.

ESSEN, OTTO VON. *Grundzüge der hochdeutschen Satzintonation.* Düsseldorf, Germany: A. Henn Verlag, 1956.

GREBE, PAUL, and MANGOLD, MAX, Editors. *Duden—Aussprachewörterbuch*, Vol. 6. Mannheim, Germany: Bibliographisches Institut, Dudenverlag, 1962.

KNIESCH, THEODOR. *Phonetikkurs, Deutsch* (text with records and tapes). New York: Goldsmith Music Shop, 1964.

MOULTON, WILLIAM G. *The Sounds of English and German.* Chicago: University of Chicago Press, 1962. (R)

RODEMEYER, FRIEDRICH KARL. *Deutsche Sprechbildung und Aussprache.* Munich and Berlin, Germany: Verlag von R. Oldenbourg, 1935.

WÄNGLER, HANS-HEINRICH. *Grundriss einer Phonetik des Deutschen mit einer allgemeinen Einführung in die Phonetik.* Marburg, Germany: N. G. Elwert Verlag, 1960.

———. *Instruction in German Pronunciation for Americans* (with tapes). St. Paul, Minn.: Educational Materials Division, 1965.

———. *Patterns in German Stress and Intonation.* St. Paul, Minn.: EMC Corporation, Educational Material Division, 1966.

General Works on German Structure (*Morphology, Syntax*)

BECH, GUNNAR. *Das semantische System der deutschen Modalverben.* Copenhagen, Denmark: "Travaux du cercle linguistique de Copenhague," *IV*, 1949.

————. *Studien über das deutsche Verbum Infinitum.* Copenhagen, Denmark: Ejnar Munksgaard, 1955–1957.

BIERWISCH, MANFRED. *Grammatik des deutschen Verbs.* Berlin, Germany: Akademie Verlag, 1963.

BOOST, KARL. *Neue Untersuchungen zum Wesen und zur Struktur des deutschen Satzes.* Berlin, Germany: Akademie Verlag, 1955.

BRINKMANN, HENNING. *Die deutsche Sprache: Gestalt und Leistung.* Düsseldorf, Germany: Schwann Verlag, 1962. (R)

CURRMÉ, GEORGE O. *A Grammar of the German Language.* Second Edition. New York: Frederick Ungar Publishing Company, 1960.

DAL, INGRID. *Kurze deutsche Syntax.* Second Edition. Tübingen, Germany: Max Niemeyer Verlag, 1962.

DRACH, ERICH. *Grundgedanken der deutschen Satzlehre.* Fourth Edition. Darmstadt, Germany: Wissenschaftliche Buchgesellschaft, 1963. (R)

ERBEN, JOHANNES. *Abriss der deutschen Grammatik.* Eighth Edition. Berlin, Germany: Akademie Verlag, 1965. (B)

FLÄMING, WALTER. *Zum Konjunktiv der deutschen Sprache der Gegenwart: Inhalte und Gebrauchsweisen.* Berlin, Germany: Akademie Verlag, 1959.

GLINZ, HANS. *Der deutsche Satz, Wortarten und Satzglieder, wissenschaftlich gefasst und dichterisch qewertet.* Düsseldorf, Germany: Schwann Verlag, 1961.

————. *Die innere Form des Deutschen: Eine neue deutsche Grammatik.* Berne, Switzerland: H. Franke A.G. 1952.

GREBE, PAUL, Editor. *Duden—Die Grammatik der deutschen Gegenwartsprache.* Second Edition, Vol. 4. Mannheim, Germany: Bibliographisches Institut, Dudenverlag, 1966.

HERMANN, PAUL, and STOLTE, HEINZ. *Kurze deutsche Grammatik.* Third Edition. Tübingen, Germany: Max Niemeyer Verlag, 1962.

HOFSTAETTER, WALTER. *Deutsche Sprachlehre.* Berlin, Germany: W. de Gruyter Verlag, 1960.

JORGENSEN, PETER. *German Grammar.* Revised and translated by F. O. RICKERING. New York: New York University Press, 1963.

JUDE, WILHELM KARL. *Deutsche Grammatik.* Tenth Edition. Braunschweig, Germany: G. Westermann Verlag, 1961.

KUFNER, HERBERT L. *The Grammatical Structures of English and German.* Chicago: University of Chicago Press, 1962. (R)

MUES, WERNER. *Vom Laut zum Satz: Die Hauptformen der deutschen Sprachstruktur. Eine einführende Uebersicht.* Heidelberg, Germany: Julius Groos Verlag, 1964.

SCHNEIDER, WILHELM. *Stilistische deutsche Grammatik: Die Stilwerte der Wortarten, der Wortstellungen und des Satzes.* Basle, Switzerland: Heider Verlag, 1959.

SCHULZ, DORA, and GRIESSBACH, HEINZ. *Grammatik der deutschen Sprache.* Munich, Germany: Max Hueber Verlag, 1960. (R)

German Vocabulary (*Synonyms, Frequency Counts, Dictionaries*)

BELLERIDGE, HAROLD T., Editor. *The New Cassell's German Dictionary.* New York: Funk and Wagnalls, 1962.

BRÜCKMANN, GEORG. *Geflügelte Worte.* Cologne, Germany: Atlas Verlag, 1950.

Duden—Bildwörterbuch der deutschen Sprache, Vol. 3. Second Edition. Mannheim, Germany: Bibliographisches Institut, Dudenverlag, 1958.

ENGEROFF, KARL, and LOVELACE-KÄUFER, CICELY. *An English-German Dictionary of Idioms.* Munich, German: Max Huber Verlag, 1960.

FARRELL, R. B. *Dictionary of German Synonyms.* Cambridge, Mass.: Cambridge University Press, 1963.

GREBE, PAUL, Editor. *Duden—Die Rechtschreibung der deutschen Sprache und der Fremdwörter,* Vol. 1. Fifteenth Edition. Mannheim, Germany: Bibliographisches Institut, Dudenverlag, 1961.

——— and MÜLLER, WOLFGANG, Editors. *Duden-Vergleichendes Synonymwörterbuch,* Vol. 8. Mannheim, Germany: Bibliographisches Institut, Dudenverlag, 1964.

——— and STREITBERG, GERHART, Editors. *Duden—Stilwörterbuch der deutschen Sprache,* Vol. 2. Fifth Edition. Mannheim, Germany: Bibliographisches Institut, Dudenverlag, 1963.

HAUCH, E. F. *German Idiom Test.* New York: The Macmillan Company, 1930.

Heath's New German and English Dictionary. Boston: D. C. Heath & Company, 1939.

JACOBS, NOAH J. *Embarrassing Moments in German and How to Avoid Them* (lists of idioms, "false cognates"). New York: Frederick Ungar Publishing Company, 1956.

MORGAN, B. Q. *A German Frequency Word Book.* New York: The Macmillan Company, 1928.

MOTEKAT, HELMUT, and BOURKE, JOHN. *Brockhaus, Illustrated German-English, English-German Dictionary.* New York: McGraw Hill Book Company, 1965.

PELTZER, KARL. *Das treffende Wort.* Munich, Germany: Ott Verlag, 1959.

PFEFFER, J. ALAN. *Grunddeutsch, Basic (Spoken) German Word List, Grundstufe.* Englewood Cliffs, N.J.: Prentice-Hall, 1965.

———. *Grunddeutsch, Index of English Equivalents for the Basic (Spoken) German Word List, Grundstufe.* Englewood Cliffs, N.J.: Prentice-Hall, 1965.

PURIN, C. M. *A Standard German Vocabulary.* Boston: D. C. Heath & Company, 1937.

Der Sprachbrockhaus. Seventh Edition. Wiesbaden, Germany: Brockhausverlag, 1966.

TAYLER, RONALD, and GOTTSCHALK, WALTER. *A German-English Dictionary of Idioms,* Second Edition. Munich, Germany: Max Huber Verlag, 1966.

WÄNGLER, HANS-HEINRICH. *Rangwörterbuch hochdeutscher Umgangssprache.* Marburg, Germany: N. G. Elwert Verlag, 1963.

German Textbooks

The books included in the following list illustrate pedagogical devices discussed in this book and show some impact of a linguistic orientation. The brief statements accompanying the titles indicate the chief reason for including the books in the list, but are not meant to be complete evaluations or endorsements.

ALLISON, DONALD E., and CARTER, BOYD G. *German Review Grammar*. New York: The Ronald Press Company, 1965.
Conversational practice and pattern drills based on reading.

BAIRMANN, HANS. *Man spricht deutsch*. New York: Goldsmith Music Shop, 1964.
Fifty-two lessons consisting of dialogues and pattern drills. Available in records.

BAUER, ERIC W., and BAUER, BRIGETT. *Lebendiges Deutsch*. New York: Holt, Rinehart and Winston, Inc., 1967
Pattern drills based on situational dialogues and reading selections. The use of traditional grammatical terminology is combined with applications of linguistic principles.

BLUSKE, MARGARET KEIDEL, and WALTHER, ELISABETH KEIDEL. *Das erste Jahr*. New York: Charles Scribner's Sons, 1965.
First-year course including structure drills and laboratory manual.

CUNZ, DIESTER, GROENKE, ULRICH A., and VAIL, CURTIS C. D. *German for Beginners*. Second Edition. New York: The Ronald Press Company, 1965.
Fairly traditional text adapted to an audio-lingual approach.

ELLERT, F. C. *German A*. Chicago: Encyclopaedia Britannica Films, 1962.
Programmed text.
————— and HELLER, PETER. *German One for Laboratory and Classroom*. Boston: D. C. Heath & Company, 1964.
One-year course based on pattern drills and special laboratory exercises.

FEHLAU, ULAND F. *Fundamental German*. Second Edition. New York: Harper & Row, 1963.
Traditional text adaptable to audio-lingual pattern approach.

GOEDSCHE, C. R., and SPANN, M. *Deutsch für Amerikaner*. Second Edition. New York: American Book Company, 1964.
Revised edition including materials for prereading instruction, pronunciation, and pattern drills.

HOFE, HAROLD V. *Der Anfang*. Revised Edition. New York: Holt, Rinehardt and Winston, 1963.
Oral drill exercises and laboratory manual.

HUEBENER, TH., and NEWARK, M. *A First Course in German*. Second Edition. Boston: D. C. Heath & Company, 1964.
Traditional text modernized through prereading lessons and oral drills.

KAHN, LOTHAR. *Intermediate Conversational German*. New York: American Book Company, 1963.
Pattern practice applied on an intermediate course stressing audio-lingual approach.

KIRCH, Max S., and MOENKEMEYER, HEINZ. *Functional German*. New York: American Book Company, 1960.
Pattern drills, English cuing of German patterns.
————— and KIESER, ROLF. *New Functional German*. New York: American Book Company, 1967.
Revision of the above title with emphasis on oral practice materials, inclusion of additional review lessons.

LEDERER, HERBERT. *Basic German: An Introduction.* New York: Charles Scribner's Sons, 1966.

Programmed approach to a systematic presentation of the similarities and differences of English and German grammar.

LEHMANN, W. P., REHDER, HELMUT, and SCHULZ-BEHREND, GEORG. *Active German.* New York: Holt, Rinehart and Winston, 1963.

Audio-lingual approach. Pattern drills based on conversations.

LOHAN, ROBERT. *A Concise German Grammar for Reference and Review.* New York: Frederick Ungar Publishing Company, 1955.

LOHNES, W. F., and STROTHMANN, F. W. *German: A Structural Approach.* New York: W. W. Norton and Company, 1967.

The text is based on a careful and modern analysis of German syntax, and features pattern practice as well as a precise comparison of German and English grammar.

MEYER, ERIKA. *Elementary German.* Boston: Houghton Mifflin Company, 1965.

A traditional text; well-organized and clear presentation of grammar.

MODERN LANGUAGE MATERIALS DEVELOPMENT CENTER (Modern Language Association of America) *Audio-lingual Materials,* Level I and Level II. New York: Harcourt Brace & World, 1961, 1962.

Audio-lingual pattern drills developed from the memorization of conversations.

MUELLER, HUGO. Three volumes: *Deutsch, Erstes Buch*; *Deutsch, Zweites Buch*; *Deutsch, Drittes Buch.* Milwaukee, Wis.: Bruce Publishing Company, 1958, 1959, 1963.

Integrated course relying especially in initial stages on conversations and pattern drills (including English wing and wall charts used as visual aids).

MULLIGAN, JOHN L. *Jetzt lesen wir (um besser zu hören, um besser zu sprechen, um besser zu schreiben).* Chicago: Scott Foresman & Company, 1965.

Intermediate reader including pattern drills and concise grammar.

PFEFFER, J. ALAN. *German Review Grammar.* Boston: D. C. Heath & Company, 1963.

Review grammar includes pattern drills and exercises encouraging creating of original sentences.

POLITZER, ROBERT L. *Toward Fluency in Reading German.* Englewood Cliffs, N.J.: Prentice-Hall, 1968.

The grammar applies the pattern recognition principle to the teaching of reading.

————. *Speaking German.* Englewood Cliffs, N.J.: Prentice-Hall, 1968.

An alternate version of the text above, emphasizing speaking through audio-lingual drills.

REHDER, HELMUT, *et al. Deutsch: Sprechen und Lesen.* New York: Holt, Rinehart and Winston, 1963.

Second-level materials, conversations, pattern practices, grammatical appendix.

————. *Deutsch: Verstehen und Sprechen.* New York: Holt, Rinehart and Winston 1962.

Elementary (first-level) high school text utilizing memorization of conversation, recombination of structure, and various types of pattern practices.

————, THOMAS, URSULA, and TWADDELL, FREEMAN. *Deutsch: Lesen und Denken.* New York: Holt, Rinehart and Winston, 1964.
Third-level course with emphasis on the development of reading and writing skills.

————, and TWADDELL, FREEMAN. *German.* Revised Edition. New York: Holt, Rinehart and Winston, 1950.
Pattern-practice oriented text utilizing memorization of basic sentences and English cuing of German patterns.

RICHARDS, I. A., *et al. German Through Pictures.* New York: Washington Square Press, 1953.
The "basic English" approach transferred to a subjectively constructed "basic German" taught with the help of visual aids (stick figures).

RIVENC, P., and GUBERINA, P. *Deutsch durch audio-visuelle Methode.* U.S. distribution: Philadelphia: Chilton Books, 1963.
Pattern practice combined with audio-visual approach and pictorial cuing of patterns.

ROGERS, R. MAX, and WATKINS, ARTHUR R. *German Through Conversational Patterns.* New York: Dodd, Mead and Company, 1967.
Twenty-four lessons featuring pattern drills, dialogues, careful grading of grammatical progression.

SCHERER, GEORGE A. C. and WÄNGLER, HANS-HEINRICH. *Contemporary German.* New York: McGraw Hill Book Company, 1966.
Combination of a traditional approach with pattern practice and simultaneous emphasis on the development of all skills.

SCHMIDT, GERARD F. *Hör gut zu.* New York: The Macmillan Company, 1965.
Elementary reader geared to aural recognition of patterns.

SCHULZ, DORA, and GRIESBACH, HEINZ. *Deutsche Sprachlehre für Amerikaner.* HAROLD VON HOFE, Editor. New York: Charles Scribner's Sons, 1965.
Special adaptation for American students on the elementary level of materials developed at the Goethe Institute. Structure drills of all types based on a careful analysis of points of difficulty for American students.

SHARP, STANLEY L., BLAUTH, HENRY, and LIEDTKE, KURT E. H. *A Solid Foundation in German.* Waltham, Mass.: Blaisdell Publishing Company, 1955.
Combination of pattern practice with traditional "paradigmatic" presentation.

SHAW, LEROY R. *Focus on German for Beginners.* New York: Harper & Row, 1965.
Pattern drills based on dialogues. Exercises dealing with intonation, pronunciation.

———— and WINTER, WERNER. *Focus on German for Intermediates.* New York: Harper & Row, 1965.
Intermediate-level text utilizing pattern drill approach.

VAN HORN, VAIL, and SPARK, KIMBERLEY. *Deutsche Grammatik, eine Ergänzung.* New York: Harcourt, Brace and World, 1967.
English-German translations, pattern drills are the main features of a step-by-step grammar review.

WEIMAR, KARL S., and HOFFMEISTER, WERNER GEORG. *Practice and Progress.*

Waltham, Mass.: Blaisdell Publishing Company, 1963.
Traditional grammar containing some pattern drills.

WEINSTEIN, ALLEN I., *et al. Deutsche Stunden.* New York: Charles Scribner's Sons, 1965.
Substitution, transformation exercises with extensive use of visual aids and visual diagramming of patterns.

Journals Dealing with Pedagogical Problems

Deutschunterricht im Ausland. Goethe Institut, Munich, Germany.

Foreign Language Annals, A Review of Current Progress in Teaching Foreign Languages. Modern Language Association of America, 60 Fifth Ave., New York.

The German Quarterly. American Association of Teachers of German, Syracuse University, Syracuse, New York.

Language Learning: A Journal of Applied Linguistics. English Language Institute, The University of Michigan, Ann Arbor, Michigan.

The Linguistic Reporter (Newsletter of the Center for Applied Linguistics), 1346 Connecticut Ave. N.W., Washington, D.C.

International Review of Applied Linguistics in Language Teaching. Julius Groos Verlag, Heidelberg, Germany.

The Modern Language Journal. National Federation of Modern Language Teachers Associations, St. Louis, Missouri.

Monatshefte für deutschen Unterricht. Department of German, University of Wisconsin, Madison, Wisconsin.